YOUR
NEIGHBOR
CELEBRATES

Your Neighbor Celebrates

by

ARTHUR GILBERT

and

OSCAR TARCOV

Foreword by

The Very Reverend JAMES A. PIKE

Book Design by

EZEKIEL SCHLOSS

FRIENDLY HOUSE PUBLISHERS

NEW YORK CITY

MANUFACTURED IN THE UNITED STATES OF AMERICA

Foreword

There is an old maxim, *Lex orandi, lex credendi,* which means roughly "people believe as they worship." Especially in those religious traditions which are liturgical and ceremonial, we can, from their accustomed round of prayer, actions, fast and festival, come nearer to the heart of the religious convictions of a people than we can from theological tomes and commentaries. For it is worship, above all, which makes its profoundest imprint upon the conscious and unconscious minds —souls—of men.

In recent years, there have been a number of efforts to help the members of different religious traditions understand each other. This is all to the good. I welcome especially, however, this small volume, because it will bring to people of all faiths, most effectively, a sense of the real meaning of Judaism. This treatment does not—and was not intended to—exhaust Judaism's meaning or cover it comprehensively, but it may lead many to go further into the theology and ethics which Hebrew worship expresses. Speaking for the Christians who will read this book, I can say that they will not only understand better the religion of many of their neighbors, but also, from its pages, they will understand their own faith better; for a man cannot be a Christian without also being a Jew in spirit. As Pope Pius XI said, "We are all Semites spiritually."

Before closing, I would like to compliment the authors and sponsors of this publication for the breadth of spirit which prompted them to make this treatment available to men of all faiths and of none. May the God of Abraham, Isaac, and Jacob, the God who is the Father of us all, bless those who read these pages.

The Very Reverend JAMES A. PIKE, J.S.D., D.D.
Dean of the Episcopal Cathedral of St. John the Divine,
New York City

Table of Contents

ACKNOWLEDGMENTS

The work of establishing better intergroup relations in America has enlisted the efforts of countless men and women of every creed. We in the Anti-Defamation League are proud to be associated with such individuals who recognize that a worship of God inevitably must compel a profounder understanding between men. It is in this spirit that we compliment the numerous Christian leaders whose educational efforts have spurred us on to create such materials as this book.

For their encouragement, support and guidance, acknowledgment is made to the following individuals associated with the interreligious advisory committee of Anti-Defamation League of B'nai B'rith: Rev. Dr. William F. Rosenblum, New York; Rev. Dr. Abraham J. Feldman, Hartford, Connecticut; Rabbi Theodore Friedman, South Orange, New Jersey; Rabbi Charles Schulman, New York. Gratitude is due to the national executive committee members of the ADL: Hon. Henry Epstein, chairman national program committee; David H. Litter, Louis Zara, vice-chairmen, national program committee; and to the following members of the administrative staff: Benjamin R. Epstein, national director and Oscar Cohen, national director, program division.

We wish to thank Benjamin Efron for his invaluable assistance with particular regard to the section on the synagogue. Thanks, too, to the Riverdale Temple, New York, the East Side Hebrew Institute, New York, and Temple Menorah, Bloomfield, New Jersey, for allowing us to photograph their ceremonial observances.

For editorial assistance, our appreciation to Judith Hershcopf and Ruth M. Schwartz of the Anti-Defamation League, and to Bernard Scharfstein.

Lastly, may we express our great indebtedness to Rabbi Irving J. Rosenbaum, upon whose earlier pamphlet part of this book is based.

HENRY EDWARD SCHULTZ
Chairman, Anti-Defamation League of B'nai B'rith

Introduction

We Americans are noted for our friendly curiosity about the ways of our neighbors. This is natural, for Americans come from every corner of the globe. Our differing customs and traditions add to the enrichment and enjoyment of our everyday life. Many books and articles have been written about the variety of religions in our country and this book is an addition to that group. It is designed to explain the customs and rituals of the Jewish religion—the faith of more than five and a half million Americans.

When this nation was first founded, George Washington declared that the privilege of worshiping God in any way one wished was both a "choice blessing" and a "precious right" of its people. That statement is as true today as it was in his time. The way in which present-day American Jews celebrate their Holy Days and festivals, the spiritual import of their observances, the character of their synagogues and temples and the significance of ceremonial objects—these are depicted in the following chapters. The photographs portray the several variations of Judaism practiced in America today — all based on an historic belief in God and trust in mankind.

Your Neighbor Celebrates incorporates the contents of two pamphlets, *Your Neighbor Celebrates* and *Your Neighbor Worships,* both originally published by the Anti-Defamation League of B'nai B'rith. Because these pamphlets have enjoyed great popularity, they have now been combined, with many additions and revisions, for use by church educators, parents, teachers and, in fact, everyone interested in acquiring authoritative information about the beliefs and practices of their Jewish neighbors.

It is our hope that this book will aid in the growth of better understanding and friendship between people of different faiths.

REV. DR. WILLIAM F. ROSENBLUM
Chairman, Interreligious Committee
Anti-Defamation League of B'nai B'rith

Rosh Hashanah

MOST of us take it for granted that New Year's Day comes on the first of January when it is cold and wintry. We also are quite sure that it never starts until midnight, and that it is a day of gay and carefree rejoicing. As a matter of fact, however, New Year's Day throughout history has been celebrated at different times of the year and day, and in different fashions.

Jewish children, with their fellow Americans, celebrate January first as the national legal New Year's holiday, but they still observe *Rosh Hashanah* as their religious New Year, just as the Bible instructs them:

"On the first day of the seventh month you shall have a holy convocation; you shall do no laborous work. It is a day for you to blow the trumpets." (Leviticus 23:24; Numbers 29:1)

Rosh Hashanah, which in Hebrew means "first of the year," comes in the autumn and begins, not at midnight, but at sunset of the day before (just as, for example, Christmas begins with Christmas Eve) and ends with sunset of the holy day itself. Rosh Hashanah is the beginning of the Jewish religious holidays called the "High Holidays," or "Days of Awe." *Yom Kippur,* the "Day of Atonement," which comes ten days after Rosh Hashanah, concludes this holy period.

According to Jewish tradition, Rosh Hashanah is the day on which God judges the deeds of every man. There is an old Jewish legend which says that on Rosh Hashanah there are three books placed before the heavenly judge. One of the books is quite thin. In it are written the names of all of the completely wicked people of the world. These very wicked people are immediately condemned on Rosh Hashanah to a year of trouble and unhappiness. Another book, which is even thinner, contains the names of those who are completely good. These people are given a year of peace and happiness. But by far the largest and thickest of the books is the one in which are written the names of those ordinary people who are neither wholly good nor wholly bad. What happens to these people, says the ancient story, is decided by the sincerity of their repentance and the way they act during the ten days which begin on Rosh Hashanah and end with Yom Kippur.

Of course this is only a legend, but it is true that on Rosh Hashanah Jewish people do resolve to live better lives. They pray for forgiveness and a year of peace and happiness for themselves and all the world.

Many people in Orthodox and Conservative synagogues celebrate Rosh Hashanah for two days in accordance with ancient tradition. Others, in Reform synagogues, observe the holiday for only one day.

While Rosh Hashanah is not accompanied by the gay merrymaking which marks January first, it is not by any means a somber or sad holiday. As a matter of fact, Jewish tradition declares that it should be a happy one, for Jews

The shofar, made from a ram's horn, calls Jews to prayer and meditation on the New Year.

are convinced that sincere prayer and good deeds find favor in the eyes of God.

At home on Rosh Hashanah eve, the family celebrates the New Year with a festive dinner. The father recites the *Kiddush,* a blessing over the holiday cup of wine, and gives some to each member of the family. One of the beautiful customs of Rosh Hashanah is the eating of an apple or some other fruit dipped in honey, to express the hope that the coming year may be full of sweetness.

On Rosh Hashanah morning, prayer services are held in the synagogue. In the most solemn part of these services, the congregation prays to God to hasten the time when all the people of the earth shall be brothers, and wickedness and tyranny shall pass away like smoke into the sky.

During the services, a section is read from the Bible. The Bible used in the synagogue does not look like an ordinary printed book. It is a parchment scroll, written by hand. When closed, it is covered with a beautiful cloth. This scroll (*Sefer Torah*) contains the first five books of the Bible in the original Hebrew. In times gone by, all books were written in this fashion. The scriptural reading assigned for Rosh Hashanah is divided into several sections, and members of the synagogue are called to the reading desk to take part in the public reading of the scripture. This is considered a great honor. The portion read on Rosh Hashanah tells the story of Abraham and Isaac. It recalls the sacrifice that Abraham, father of the Hebrew people, was willing to make in order to demonstrate his devotion to the Lord. The story reminds the congregation that they, too, must renew their faith.

Of course, the prayers and Bible reading are an important part of Rosh Hashanah. But if you were to ask any Jewish youngster what he thought was the most important ceremony of the day, he would certainly reply, "the blowing of the

"Come before the Lord with singing."

shofar." The *shofar* is made from the horn of a ram. It has a loud and piercing sound and was used in ancient Israel to call the people together for emergencies or for peaceful assemblies. In the synagogue on Rosh Hashanah, the call of the shofar reminds the congregation of the need for doing good and for living an honorable and God-fearing life. The striking cry of the ram's horn calls upon worshippers to repent any misdeeds.

Often the prayers are chanted in Hebrew, the language in which the Old Testament was written, and in which men prayed during the time of Jesus. Nowadays in almost all synagogues, some prayers are recited in English, too. This is done so that everyone, whether he knows Hebrew or not, may take part in the services. Many High Holiday prayer books contain English translations alongside the Hebrew text so that even though the cantor or congregation may be reciting the Hebrew, everyone can follow and understand.

Among the very stirring prayers recited during the service is the litany:

> *Our Father, our King, hear our prayer*
> *Our Father, our King, we have sinned before Thee.*
> *Our Father, our King, have mercy upon us and upon our children.*
> *Our Father, our King, keep far from our country pestilence, war and famine.*
> *Our Father, our King, cause all hate and oppression to vanish from the earth.*
> *Our Father, our King, inscribe us for blessing in the book of life.*
> *Our Father, our King, grant unto us a year of happiness . . .*
> *Our Father, our King, be merciful and answer us; though we plead no merit, deal with us according to Thy loving-kindness and help us.*
> *Amen.*

*At the most solemn moment in the Rosh Hashanah ceremony,
the cantor kneels before the Holy Ark.*

Yom Kippur

YOM KIPPUR (the Day of Atonement) is the last day of the "Ten Days of Penitence" which begin with Rosh Hashanah. This ten-day period, according to Jewish tradition, is a time for repentance, prayer and charity in preparation for the holiest day of the year, Yom Kippur. On this solemn and important day almost all Jewish men and women refrain from eating and drinking, and even young children try to fast for at least a part of the day. The Bible (Leviticus 16: 29-31; 23: 26-31; Numbers 29: 7) also requires that Jews do no manner of work on Yom Kippur. The people spend the entire day in prayer and worship.

The word "atonement" explains the nature of the day. For "atonement" is made up of two words — "at" and "one." And

The notes sounded on the shofar signify the sadness, joy and hope in life.

9

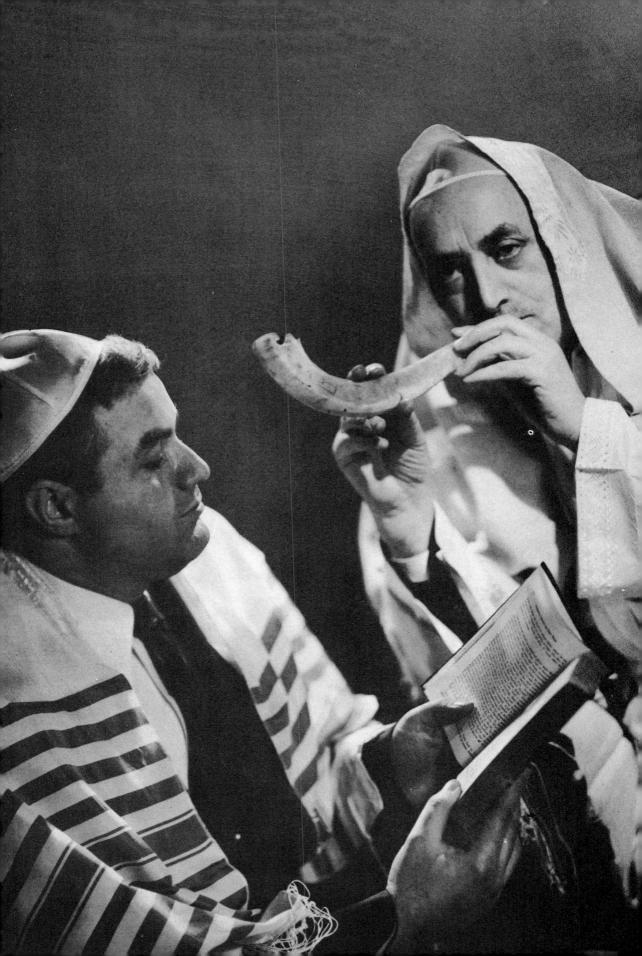

on the day of "at-one-ment" Jewish people seek to be "at-one" — in harmony with God. Yom Kippur is, above all, a day on which Jews seek forgiveness not only from God, but also from man. Judaism teaches that one cannot ask God's forgiveness for wrong-doing unless he has also asked others to forgive him for any evil he may have done to them. But simply asking for forgiveness is not enough. The wrong must be righted whenever that is possible. There must be a true feeling of repentance. God recognizes the sincere desire of the worshipper to undo his evil and to live his life better.

Just as the best-known part of the Rosh Hashanah service is the blowing of the shofar, so in the Yom Kippur services, the part best-known and loved by the Jewish young people is the famous *Kol Nidre* prayer. This Kol Nidre prayer is recited on the eve of the holiday. It is not so much the words of the prayer which are stirring, but the awesome and inspiring melody. This beautiful melody has become so much a part of the world's great religious music that singers and musicians of many faiths have made recordings of it. The prayer itself asks God to forgive the congregation for breaking any religious vows made to Him which they might not be able to fulfil. (In fact, *Kol Nidre* means "all vows.") If a man tries his best to fulfil his vows unto the Lord, but is prevented from so doing through no fault of his own, the Kol Nidre allows him to be at peace once more with his conscience and with God. The prayer does not apply to promises between one man and another. These cannot be broken except by the consent of the person to whom the promise is made.

Yom Kippur eve is observed in the synagogue in solemn and serious fashion with prayers and hymns. Below is one of the more beautiful prayers recited in many synagogues on Yom Kippur eve.

11

> *O Lord, our God, let Thy presence be manifest to us in all Thy works, that reverence for Thee may fill the hearts of all Thy creatures. May all the children of men come before Thee in humility and unite to do Thy will with perfect heart, that all may acknowledge that Thine are power, dominion and majesty, and that Thy name is exalted above all.*

Late in the evening, most members of the congregation return to their homes from the synagogue; some very pious people spend the entire night in prayer. Services are held all the next day, beginning with early morning and ending at nightfall.

One of the important Bible readings in the synagogue on Yom Kippur is taken from the Book of Isaiah:

> *Is not this the fast that I have chosen?*
> *To loose the fetters of wickedness,*
> *To undo the bonds of the yoke,*
> *And to let the oppressed go free . . .*
> *Is it not to deal thy bread to the hungry*
> *And that thou bring the homeless to thy house?*
> *When thou seest the naked, that thou cover him,*
> *And that thou hide not thyself from thy fellow man.*
> *Then shall thy light break forth as the morning . . .*
> *And thy righteousness shall go before thee.*

The prophet Isaiah declares that the fast of Yom Kippur is acceptable to God only if it leads to good deeds towards man. This is the lesson Yom Kippur teaches.

Also conducted on this Holy Day is the *Yizkor,* a memorial service for the departed. This service reminds those whose dear ones have passed away to follow the path of righteousness and to remember the good deeds of their departed.

The concluding prayers of the day are recited towards sunset. At nightfall, the end of the fast is announced by a single blast of the shofar, after which the worshippers return to their homes joyous and glad of heart.

Succoth

FOUR days after Yom Kippur comes the most joyous of Jewish holidays, *Succoth,* a festival celebrating the time when the ancient Israelites gathered in their fruit harvest and offered thanks to God for His goodness. In many ways it is similar to the American Thanksgiving, and some scholars believe that the Pilgrim fathers were inspired to hold their first Thanksgiving by the Succoth festival about which they read in the Bible.

During the nine days of this holiday, many Jews eat their meals and spend part of their time in a *succah* (a little booth or hut with an open roof of branches and leaves). These booths commemorate the temporary shelters in which the ancient Israelites lived on their journey from Egypt to the Promised Land. It is the succah, too, that gives the holiday its name; in English, Succoth is frequently called the "Feast of Booths."

In bygone days, it was customary for each Jewish family to build its own succah, but today, with smaller families and city living, it has become more usual for the members of a synagogue to build one large succah for the entire congregation.

Children delight in decorating the succah with colorful fall fruits and vegetables.

Everyone, young and old, takes part in building the succah, but it is usually the children who are given the pleasant task of decorating it with colorful fall fruits and vegetables. Fragilely constructed, the succah is meant to remind man that his salvation depends not upon material things, which are at best, transitory, but upon the Lord, who is eternal. It is for this reason, too, that the roof of the succah is left partly open. Thus, a man may look up at the stars and direct his thoughts heavenward.

If you were to visit a synagogue on Succoth, your eye would immediately be caught by the array of long green palm branches and bright yellow citrons, a lemon-like fruit of the Holy Land. The palm branch (*lulav*) is held in one hand together with a few sprigs of myrtle and willow, while the citron (*ethrog*) is held in the other. These are waved in all directions during part of the service to show that God, who is being thanked for His gifts of the harvest, is found everywhere. This ceremony is based on the words of Leviticus 23:40: "And ye shall take you on the first day the fruit of goodly trees, branches of palm trees, and boughs of thick trees and willows of the brook, and ye shall rejoice before the Lord your God seven days."

The rabbis used to suggest that these symbols taught man a lesson about brotherhood. According to the old legend, the tall palm leaves depicted a person who was proud, the drooping willow branches one who was humble, the lovely myrtle a person who had beautiful qualities but little accomplishment, and the fragrant citron a person who was abundant in good deeds. The true brotherhood of man, according to

Children, too, share in the Succoth observance of waving palm branches and savoring the fragrance of the citron.

15

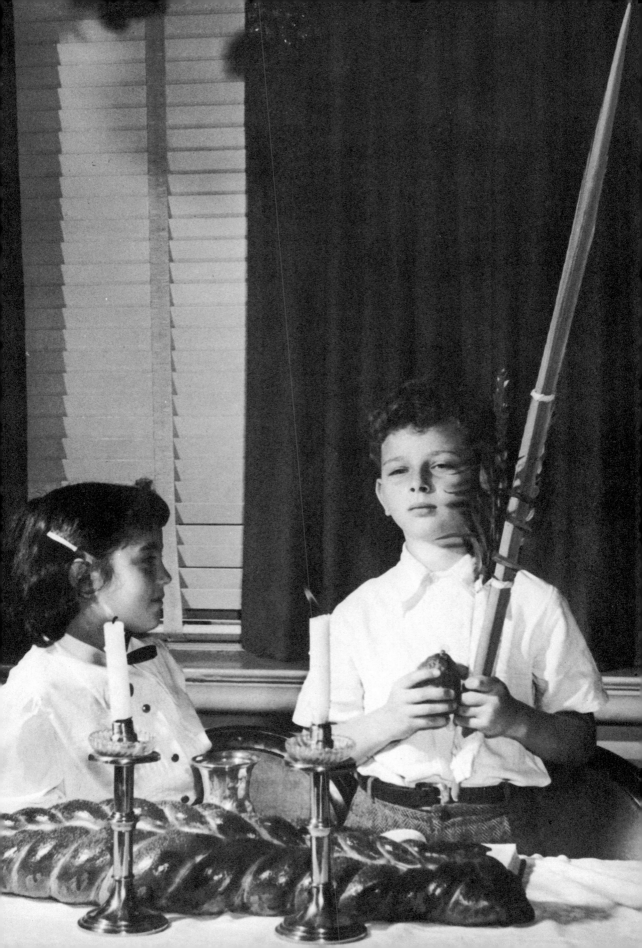

the rabbis, was the result of all such persons living together in harmony.

The first two days of Succoth are observed by Orthodox and Conservative Jews as full holidays, with special prayers and Biblical readings recited in the synagogue; Reform congregations observe only the first day as a full holiday. The next five days of Succoth are called *Hol-hamoed,* the "weekdays" of the holiday, which simply means that although special prayers are said in the synagogue on those days, Jewish children and adults may return to their workaday tasks.

It is customary to read from the Book of Ecclesiastes during the Hol-hamoed period. Like the holiday itself, this book of the Bible reminds us that it is only by trusting in the Lord that man is able to make sense of his life and give it meaning.

The seventh day of Succoth is observed as *Hoshana Rabba* (the great hosannas). According to Orthodox tradition, the final judgment of man by God, begun during Rosh Hashanah, is completed on this day. Thus, Orthodox Jews join solemn prayers from the High Holy Days to the festive prayers of Succoth. With lulav and ethrog in hand, they march around the synagogue seven times singing *hosannas,* the prayers for salvation.

The eighth day of Succoth is celebrated with a festival called *Shemini Atzereth* (the eighth day of assembly). On this day, no matter how stormy the weather outside, the congregation offers a special prayer for rain. This prayer may be traced back to ancient Israel, where Succoth marked the end of the annual dry season and the people would pray for rain and good crops in the coming year. After the morning service, people take leave of the succah and all the fruit and decorations which adorned it are given to the children or to the needy.

The succah's fragile and temporary construction reminds Jews that they must place their trust, not in material things, but in God.

Simhath Torah

FLAGS . . . songs . . . candles . . . parades . . . laughter . . . these are the sights and sounds that announce the arrival of *Simhath Torah,* the time of "rejoicing in the Torah."

Each Sabbath of the year, a section of the Torah, the sacred scrolls of Jewish law and teaching, is read aloud in the synagogue. On the ninth and final day of Succoth, the year's reading is completed. This day is known as Simhath Torah, a full-fledged holiday in itself—and a most happy one—for it celebrates the end of the year's reading and the beginning of the new.

On Simhath Torah eve, the very last part of the Torah, the closing chapter of the Book of Deuteronomy, is read aloud. This dramatic event is heralded by a procession in which the sacred scrolls are carried around the synagogue, while the children merrily follow with banners, candles and songs. The next morning another procession takes place and the scripture reading is begun anew with the first chapter of Genesis.

For the children, one of the most exciting events of the day

Simhath Torah teaches that the study of God's word is an unending process.

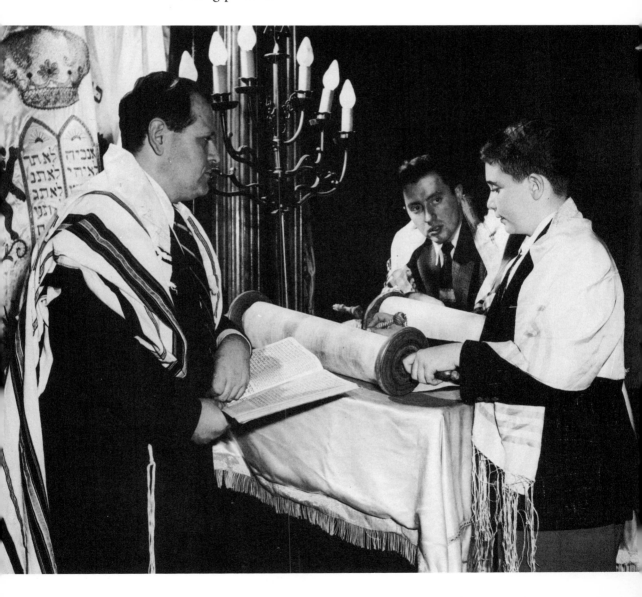

is being called to the reading desk to recite part of the Scriptures aloud. On other holidays and the Sabbath, only adults are so honored. In Reform congregations, where Simhath Torah and Shemini Atzereth are celebrated together on one day, it is customary to invite all the children just enrolled in religious school to appear before the open Ark where the scrolls are kept. There they receive their first lesson from the Torah. Afterwards, they are frequently given gifts of miniature Torah scrolls, Bibles, or chocolate goodies as symbols of the sweetness and majesty of the Torah.

Simhath Torah demonstrates that the study of God's word is an unending process. Through all of his life, man may find inspiration and guidance from the word of God. That is why the Jews treasure the Torah as their most precious possession.

Flags . . . songs . . . candles . . . parades . . . laughter . . . mark the "birthday" of the Torah.

Hanukkah

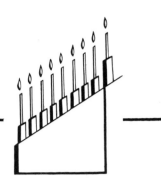

IN December of every year, Jews observe a festival called *Hanukkah*. It is a joyous holiday, celebrating the first great victory for religious freedom won by the Jews more than two thousand years ago.

In those days, the Jews of Palestine were dominated by the rule of Antiochus IV, a Syrian-Greek emperor who demanded that everyone in his empire follow his ways of worship. Attempting to force the Jews to adopt his pagan ways, he seized their temple in Jerusalem, filled it with idols and then ordered the Jews to abandon their faith on pain of death.

But the Jews refused to give up their faith in the One God. Mattathias, the elder of the town of Modin in Palestine, in defiance of the tyrant, called on the Jews to revolt. They followed their leader into the hills of Judea where Judah Maccabee, one of Mattathias' five sons, organized them into an army. Judah was called the *maccabee,* which means "hammer," because of

"Kindling new the holy lamps. . ."

the blows he struck for freedom.

For three years the Jews fought the army of Antiochus. The account of this struggle is recorded in the Book of Maccabees. There is one story that tells how the Maccabees, much smaller in number and arms than the enemy force, set up a dummy camp. The Syrian-Greeks, believing this to be the complete Jewish encampment, attacked in full force—only to find themselves surrounded by the major part of the Hebrew army, which, under cover of darkness, had left the dummy camp and encircled the entire area. (George Washington, who had studied the Book of Maccabees, used this same stratagem against the British when the outnumbered American troops were also struggling to achieve independence.)

Judah Maccabee was finally able to lead his troops victoriously into Jerusalem. There, the Jews cleansed and purified the Temple of every pagan object that had been brought into it, and made it once again a house for the worship of God. It is told in Jewish legend that when Judah's men were cleaning out the Temple, they found just a single jar of holy oil— only enough to keep the Eternal Light before the Holy Ark burning for one day. Miraculously, this one jar burned for eight days and nights.

Judah Maccabee then proclaimed an eight-day holiday to celebrate the rededication of the Temple to God. Thus the festival received its name, for Hanukkah means "dedication."

It is generally agreed by scholars that if Judaism had been defeated by the Syrian-Greeks, the religious foundations upon which Christianity was later established would have been lost to the world, and neither Judaism nor Christianity would have exerted their influence upon civilization.

Today, children love this holiday, not only because it has become a time for the giving of small gifts—very often dis-

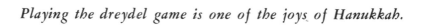
Playing the dreydel game is one of the joys of Hanukkah.

tributed on each of the eight nights—but also because Hanuk-kah is the traditional time for playing the *dreydel* game. The dreydel is a small four-sided wooden or metal top that is spun by hand. The sides are inscribed with the four Hebrew letters which begin the words: *Nes gadol haya sham* (A great miracle happened there).

It is also traditional to serve *latkes,* a kind of potato pancake, at Hanukkah parties. But the big event of Hanukkah is the candle-lighting ceremony commemorating the light that burned for eight days during the rededication of the Temple. Every night of the festival, the father of the family places candles in a special candelabrum called the *Menorah.* In the presence of the whole family he lights one candle the first night, two the second, and so on until eight candles are lit on the last night—always using a helper candle called the *Shamos.* The *b'raha* or blessing recited during the candle-lighting cere-mony reads as follows:

> *Blessed art Thou, O Lord, our God, Ruler of the universe, who has sanctified us by Thy commandments and com-manded us to kindle the light of Hanukkah.*

With the centuries, the Hanukkah candles have taken on a deep meaning for the Jews. They symbolize the light of religi-ous freedom that Judah Maccabee and his followers kept alive. And in the glow of the candles, many Jews rededicate them-selves to the ideals of their faith—as once the Maccabees rededi-cated the Temple to the service of the One God.

Because Hanukkah symbolizes the triumph of faith in God over brute force, it has long been a source of inspiration to the weak and small in number who fight for liberty and justice, against stronger and tyrannical foes. It strengthens the convic-tion that religious freedom is the right of every people and that God desires man to worship Him in freedom.

Teen-agers reenact the miracle of Hanukkah, when a single jar of holy oil burned continuously for eight days.

Hamishah Asar Bishvat

O N the fifteenth day of the Hebrew month of *Shvat,* which falls in January or February by our modern calendar, many Jewish children observe the holiday of *Hamishah Asar Bishvat,* the new year of the trees.

In ancient Palestine, when trees were abundant, it was the custom on this day for a father to plant a cedar sapling for a male child born during the year, and a cypress for a female child. At marriage, the respective trees would be cut down and used as posts for the traditional wedding canopy. But during the many centuries when the Jews were away from Palestine, the trees were destroyed and no new ones planted, until the once-fertile land became a desolate desert.

Today, in Palestine, everyone recognizes the importance of replenishing the country's trees. More than just beautifying the country, they give shade and shelter; provide such fruit as pomegranates, almonds, dates, figs, oranges, lemons and grape-fruits; protect the people from the hot, dry winds that sweep

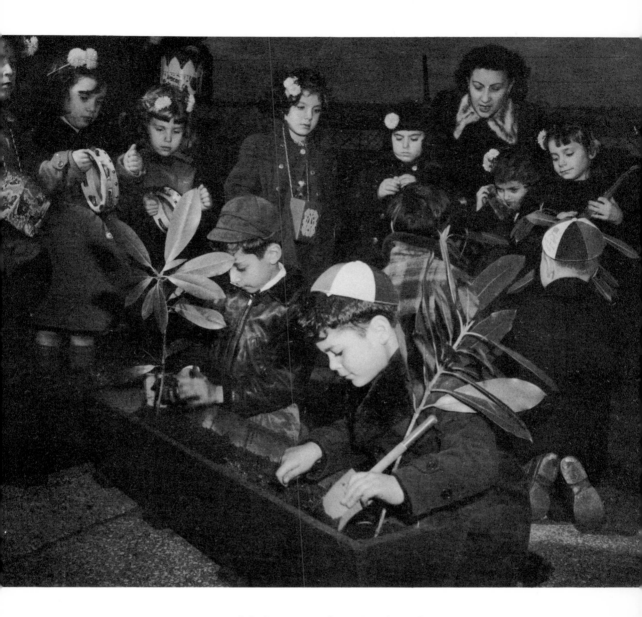

Hamishah Asar Bishvat is a day of planting new trees.

across the country; prevent the soil from eroding; provide lumber for the new homes constantly being built and help to drain the swamp lands.

Thus in present-day Israel, Hamishah Asar Bishvat has become a day of planting new trees. The children are given the privilege of doing the planting and the ceremony is followed by cheerful parties. Jewish children in America observe this holiday by partaking of a variety of Palestinian fruits—such as the ones mentioned above—and also the ancient carob or St. John's Bread, a dry pod with a sweetish pulp that still grows in Israel. In many Hebrew schools, on this day, the lessons are devoted to the study of Israel's geography and agricultural products.

Folk dancing is part of the fun of the holiday celebration.

Purim

THE story of *Purim*, as told in the Book of Esther, reads like a fairy-tale. It takes us back some twenty-four hundred years to the land of Persia, ruled by a king named Ahasuerus, where there lived a wicked man named Haman. As Prime Minister and a special favorite of the king, Haman became more proud and vain with each passing day. So vain did he become, that he commanded that everyone who passed must bow down before him.

One man alone refused to bow to Haman. That man was a Jew named Mordecai, who declared, "I bend the knee before God alone, the only living One in Heaven above." Hearing

Many centuries ago, sacred Hebrew writings were prepared on parchment scrolls. This ancient Megillah tells the story of Queen Esther's heroism.

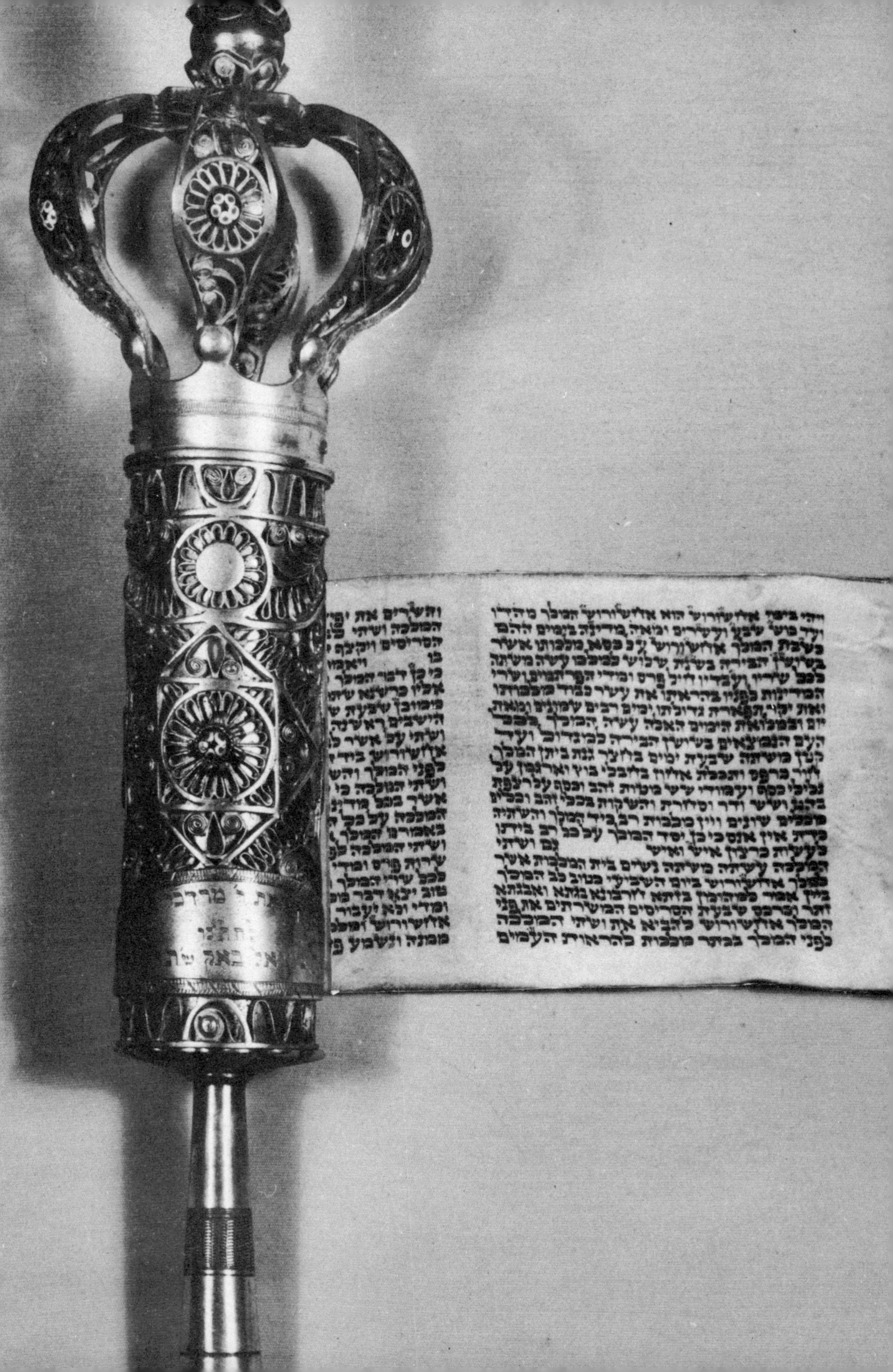

this, Haman was so angry that he decided to kill not only Mordecai, but *all* the Jews in the Persian empire. He then went to the King, and tricked him into giving his seal of approval to the evil plan.

At that time, the Queen of Persia was Esther, a Jewish lady whose great beauty had attracted King Ahasuerus. Orphaned at an early age, Esther had been brought up by Mordecai, who was her cousin. Now, as she learned from him what was about to befall her defenseless people, at great risk to her own life, she summoned up courage to ask the King for help. When Ahasuerus heard the full story, he was furious at Haman for having deceived him. But since he had already signed the decree giving Haman's men permission to attack the Jews, the only way he could help was to command that the Jews be allowed to arm and defend themselves. With God's help they did this successfully—while Ahasuerus had Haman put to death on the very gallows the Prime Minister had intended for Mordecai.

It was Haman who really named the holiday. Eager to choose the best day for his evil plan, and being superstitious, he threw lots, a kind of dice known as *purim* in Hebrew. The numbers on the lots were thirteen and twelve, which he interpreted as the thirteenth day of the twelfth month, *Adar*. He therefore commanded that the massacre be carried out on that day. When the thirteenth of Adar came, however, the Jews were prepared; the next day they celebrated their victory. Ever since that time, the holiday has been called Purim. It is celebrated on the fourteenth day of Adar, which falls in February or March on the modern calendar.

On Purim eve in the synagogue, it is traditional to read the

Queen Esther pleads for the lives of her people in a teen-age Purim play.

35

Book of Esther (in Hebrew, the *Megillah*). At every mention of Haman's name, the children stamp, clap and make all manner of noise with their Purim *greggers* (noisemakers). In this fashion, they symbolically blot out Haman's name and the memory of his evil. The next morning when the reading is concluded, the Jewish people, with prayers of thanksgiving, express their gratitude that faith proved triumphant over hatred.

In many ways, Purim has the spirit of a social event; there are carnivals and parties, costume plays and dances, and—last but not least—*hamantashen,* delicious three-cornered pastries, intriguingly filled with jam or poppy seeds.

But although Purim is a day of triumph, the Jews realize, amid all their gaiety, that Haman's defeat was but a temporary one. For in every age, they have witnessed how selfish men eager for power have tried to destroy whatever people or groups stood in their way. In their hunger, these dictators forget the law of God and spread hate and distrust, turning one people against another. Purim is a happy reminder, however, that while evil may seem all-powerful at times, it can be defeated if people of good faith work together.

Purim is a spirited holiday, with carnivals and parties, costume plays and dances.

Passover

To find the beginnings of the story of Passover (*Pesah,* in Hebrew), we must travel back thousands of years to the land of Egypt. There, the Book of Exodus tells us, the Jews were enslaved by a heartless Pharaoh. Taking pity on His people, God chose Moses to lead the Jews out of slavery. First Moses implored the Pharoah to let the Jews worship the Lord in freedom. But Pharoah refused.

The Lord then sent one plague after another upon the Egyptians until they reluctantly allowed the Hebrews to leave. He then commanded the Red Sea to open so that Hebrew slaves might escape the pursuing Egyptians and go on to a new life. Once safely encamped on dry land, the thankful Jews offered up praise to God for their deliverance. Having tasted the bitterness of slavery, they thrilled at the challenge of liberty.

So important is the emancipation story, that the whole Pass-

Passover is a family holiday, celebrated with a Seder in the home.

over ceremony is built around it. On Passover eve, the entire family gathers at the dinner table for the traditional *Seder*. Both a meal and a worship service, the Seder is celebrated with prayers, songs and blessings performed in a given order. In fact, *seder* is the Hebrew word for "order." Every member of the family, no matter where he may live, tries to be home for this important occasion. Almost always, there are guests at the table, for it is a custom to share the blessings of the holiday with friends, neighbors and even strangers who are unable to get to their own home.

Among Orthodox and Conservative Jews, the Seder is held on both the first and second nights of the eight-day holiday. Reform Jews, who observe a seven-day Passover, usually hold their own Seder on the first evening. Many synagogues now also conduct a Seder for their entire congregation.

The appointed order for the Seder ceremonies is contained in the *Haggadah*, an ancient book whose oldest portions date back at least twenty-five hundred years. Haggadah itself is the Hebrew word for "telling," and the Passover service is based on the Biblical injunction: "Thou shalt tell thy son in that day saying, 'It is because of that which the Lord did for me when I came forth out of Egypt.'" (Exodus 13:8)

Thus children play an important part in the Seder service. In fact, the service opens with the youngest son asking four questions of his father, beginning with the famous, *Ma Nish-tanah*, "Why is this night different from all other nights?" It is the father's answers that unfold the drama of the Exodus. And in the telling of the familiar but ever-stirring story of Moses and the Israelites, modern Jews, young and old, relive the anguish and joy of their forefathers. They bless the Lord, "who hath preserved us and sustained us and brought us to this season," and praise Him for the glory of each new springtime, the season when Passover is celebrated.

*Foods and ceremonial objects help **retell** the story of the Jews' liberation from slavery.*

The Seder is a meal as well as a religious service, and very special foods adorn the table. Arranged on a platter are:

matzoth—wafers of unleavened bread

maror—bitter herbs

haroseth—a mixture of chopped apples, nuts, cinnamon and wine

the shank bone of a lamb

a roasted egg

parsley or watercress

Each of these foods has a particular significance to the Jewish people, reminding them of some event, sweet or bitter, in their deliverance from slavery. As the story is retold and the foods eaten, their meaning is revealed. The unleavened matzoth represent the bread which the Jews ate on their hurried flight from Egypt, when they fled with such haste that they could not wait for the bread to leaven. The bitter herbs are a reminder of the bitterness of slavery. The mixture of chopped apples, nuts, cinnamon and wine represents the mortar with which the Jews made the bricks for Pharaoh's great cities. The shank bone is a reminder of the paschal lamb which was offered as a sacrifice in the Temple of Jerusalem during the spring pilgrimage of the earliest Hebrews. The roasted egg is a symbol of the free-will offering that accompanied the sacrifice of the paschal lamb. The parsley or watercress reminds everyone of the continual rebirth of growing things, and is a token of gratitude to God for the products of the earth that come to life each spring.

As in most Jewish ceremonies, wine is a part of the ritual, and a cup of sweet wine is placed at each setting. If desired, unfermented raisin wine may be substituted. During the service, at the mention of each of the ten plagues, the celebrants dip off part of their wine. They do this since wine symbolizes happiness, and they want to show that their happiness is incomplete. Thus the Jewish people express their sadness that some Egyptians had to suffer before freedom was granted to the Hebrew slaves.

Placed in the very center of the table is a goblet of wine called "Elijah's cup." Orthodox Jews believe that the prophet Elijah will foretell the coming of the Messiah. By filling this cup with wine, they welcome his presence at the Seder, and thereby express their hope that the promise of a Messianic Age, when all men will be at one with God and with each other, will someday be fulfilled. This custom is also retained by Conservative and Reform Jews.

Earlier in the service, one of the three matzoth on the ceremonial platter is divided in half and hidden away while the youngsters keep their eyes tightly closed. Later, the children make a spirited search for the matzah, and the lucky finder only gives it up when he has been promised a gift in exchange. This piece of matzah is called the *afikomen*—from a Greek word relating to "dessert"—because it concludes the meal. Once the afikomen has been eaten, no other food is served. When the ancient Hebrews worshipped at the Temple in Jerusalem, they would reserve a small portion of the sacrificial lamb for the close of the meal. After the Temple was destroyed and the custom of sacrifice abandoned, a piece of matzah was substituted. This is the origin of the afikomen.

As the family participates in the Seder service and meal, they sit in a relaxed position. Often a pillow is placed in the father's chair. They do this because in ancient times free men ate in a reclining position whereas slaves had to sit erect and eat hurriedly.

Probably the most beloved of all Jewish festivals, Passover is rich in songs and poems and stories. One of the most delightful songs is *Had Gadyah*—"One Kid." It is a round, sung at the conclusion of the service, that tells the tale of a kid bought by a father for his son for two *zuzim* (coins). The little goat suffers a tragic fate, but the song's tale of woe is ended by an act of God who destroys evil. So the song, like the holiday itself, teaches faith in the future, and encourages a reliance on God's promise of freedom.

Commemorating a great event in Jewish history, Passover combines beautiful ritual with family warmth and youthful fun. As a festival of freedom, it has inspired the imagination of artists and writers—both Jew and non-Jew—for many centuries. Indeed, it has inspired the hearts of all men.

Perhaps its universal significance is best expressed in the final benediction of the Passover Seder:

> *The Passover service is now completed. With songs of praise we have lifted up the cup, symbolizing the divine promises of salvation, and we have called upon the name of God. Let us again, lift our soul to God in faith and hope. May He who broke Pharaoh's yoke, forever shatter all fetters of oppression and hasten the day when swords shall at last be broken, and wars ended. Soon may He cause the glad tidings of redemption to be heard in all lands so that mankind — freed from violence and from wrong and united in an eternal confidence of brotherhood — may celebrate the universal Passover in the name of our God of Freedom. . . .*

"Why is this night different from all other nights?"

45

Lag B'Omer

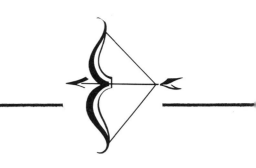

Lag B'Omer recalls the bravery of the Jewish scholars of the second century who fought for their right to study and observe God's law at the time when the Roman Emperor Hadrian had forbidden these practices under penalty of death. By doing this, Hadrian hoped to end the religious faith of the Jews which led them to despise any form of tyranny. But his oppressive laws only provoked the Jews to further rebellion.

For three years, under the brave leadership of Bar-Kochba, the Jews fought the Romans with great courage, but they could not hold out against the vast Roman army. Finally, Bar-Kochba was killed and the saintly leader of the scholars, Rabbi Akiba, was taken prisoner.

However, Akiba's favorite student, Simeon Bar Yohai, was able to win the special privilege of visiting his old teacher in prison. Unable to contain his swelling anger at the Romans' treatment of the old Rabbi and the other Jews, Simeon Bar Yohai one day spoke out against the Romans and had to flee for his life. For thirteen years he lived with his son in a mountain cave in Galilee. And for thirteen years, his only food was the fruit of the carob tree (also known as St. John's Bread) and water from a nearby stream. During those years of lonely study and contemplation, he deepened his knowledge and understanding of God and His work.

Soon many students came to visit Yohai, risking their lives for the sake of study. To avoid suspicion, they would disguise themselves as hunters and carry bows and arrows. In memory of these courageous scholars, Jewish school children today frequently plan outings and picnics on Lag B'Omer, often making bows and arrows to carry with them.

It is customary on this holiday to recall the tales of Simeon Bar Yohai's life and to think upon his teachings as written in the book, the *Zohar*, the book of "splendor." It is told, for example, that one day after many years of hiding, Rabbi Yohai saw a bird repeatedly escape a net set for it by a hunter. He took this to be an omen that God would not forsake him and he, too, left his hiding place to preach God's word openly. Soon thereafter, Emperor Hadrian died and Simeon Bar Yohai was freed from the death penalty. His sign from God had come true.

Later, he went on a mission to Rome to petition for the removal of Hadrian's oppressive laws. As a result, the new Emperor granted the Jewish people the right to continue their sacred studies.

Among Simeon Bar Yohai's sayings that still have meaning for people today are:

"So great is the power of repentance that a man who has been wicked during his lifetime, if he repents toward the end, is considered a perfectly righteous man."

"One should rather throw himself into a burning furnace than shame a neighbor in public."

Lag B'Omer, which, in Hebrew means the thirty-third day

after Passover, was the name given to the holiday in honor of Simeon Bar Yohai, who passed away on that day. His last request to his disciples was that the day of his death be observed by celebration rather than by mourning. In Israel the celebration of Simeon Bar Yohai's death is known as the *Hillula* (wedding) of Rabbi Simeon Bar Yohai. The Orthodox groups in Israel believe that just before he died, he received a revelation from God concerning the wedding of man to the universe.

On this holiday, therefore, pious Jews come from all parts of Israel and neighboring countries to honor their teacher and the ideals for which he stood. They chant psalms, sing religious songs, and climax the festivities with a huge bonfire lit at midnight. Men, young and old, sing and dance around the fire until early morning. So in Israel on this holiday the black sky of night blazes with fire, symbolic of man's passion for God's truth.

In many lands, Lag B'Omer is considered a particularly happy day for wedding celebrations.

Shavuoth

ARRIVING just as spring is about to turn into summer, *Shavuoth* (the Festival of Weeks) is a holiday of three-fold joy and pleasure. First celebrated in Biblical days as the conclusion of the grain harvest, in later years Shavuoth was identified as the holiday commemorating the revelation of the Ten Commandments to Moses at Sinai. Still more recently, Shavuoth has been established by Reform Jews as the day for the holding of confirmation ceremonies.

In those ancient times when the holiday was a simple harvest festival, it was customary to bring to the Temple at Jerusalem, as an offering to God, two loaves of bread baked from the wheat of the new crop. From Shavuoth to Succoth, an unending parade of Jewish families would come to the Temple to offer their first fruits in thanksgiving. Today in the synagogue, it is customary to read from the Book of Ruth, which tells, in part, how the Hebrew farmer was instructed by God to leave a corner of his field and the gleanings for the poor and needy.

As the holiday became recognized as the time of the giving

At Shavuoth, many Jewish boys and girls renew the promise of their forefathers to obey the Ten Commandments.

of the Law, it attained a more spiritual stature. Thus, on Shavuoth eve, many people observe the holiday by reading the Bible and studying other religious books. The Book of Ruth is also related to this phase of the holiday, since it tells how Ruth, a non-Jew, embraced Judaism and its Commandments. In all synagogues, the Ten Commandments are publicly read at the morning service.

One of the prettiest Shavuoth customs is the decoration of house and synagogue with plants and flowers. The greens recall the green mountain of Sinai, where the Commandments were given, as well as the fruits of the ancient harvest festival.

Shavuoth was chosen for the confirmation ceremony because at the time of confirmation, Jewish boys and girls renew the promise of their forefathers to obey the Ten Commandments and the teachings of the Jewish religion. In our present day, the celebration of Shavuoth directs most of its attention to the meaning of God's revelation and the importance of communicating these ideals to each generation.

Tisha B'Av

ONE of the saddest days in the Jewish calendar is *Tisha B'Av* (the ninth day of the month of *Av*). On this day, not once, but thrice did terrible disaster befall the Jewish people. The first calamity came more than 2000 years ago, in 586 B.C.E., when the Babylonians destroyed the First Temple built by King Solomon in Jerusalem. Six hundred years later, on the very same day, the Second Temple, built by Ezra and Nehemiah, was destroyed by the Roman legions. And in 1492, the very year Columbus discovered America, the Jewish people were driven from their homes in Spain by the Spanish Inquisition.

In all of these instances, thousands upon thousands of Jews perished, while untold numbers were captured as slaves. With the Roman victory, the Jews were driven from Jerusalem and compelled to wander across the face of the earth. Almost everywhere they went, they were persecuted and denied rights given to other citizens. The Jews were frequently denied employment, forbidden to own property, prevented from having any voice in the law. Even where they were able to establish great centers of learning, as they did in Spain, their lives were insecure. The Spanish rulers and their religious leaders banished from their land all people who refused to accept the faith practiced in Spain. People had not yet learned that a man could have a different religion and still be a good neighbor and citizen.

Thus, with the years, Tisha B'Av became not only a day of mourning for the destruction of the Temples, but also a day of lamentation for the endless wanderings and hardships of the Jewish people.

On Tisha B'Av eve, the synagogue is usually dark, illuminated only by the dim light of a few candles. While the worshippers sit like mourners, the official reader chants from the Book of Lamentations and many other prayers and poems are recited. Even the curtains before the Ark containing the holy Torah scroll are removed, symbolizing that the Torah, too, is in mourning for these great calamities in Jewish history. The services continue all through the following day, which is observed as a fast day by Orthodox and Conservative Jews.

Yet, sad as the service is, the gloom is not unrelieved. Here and there, rays of hope pierce the darkness. For the Orthodox Jew believes that the Messiah will be born on the ninth of Av, and the Sabbath following the fast is called the Sabbath of Comfort. Prayers and readings of consolation are heard in the synagogue on this Sabbath—including the portion of the Torah beginning with the words of Isaiah 40: "Comfort ye, comfort ye, my people, saith the Lord." Thus, in the midst of his unhappiness, the Jew recalls that God is a loving comforter.

In recent years, Tisha B'Av has lost much of its tragic overtones. While the Jewish people still look back with compassion at the hard lives of their forefathers, they are overjoyed that freedom is flourishing in so many parts of the world.

In the midst of the sadness of Tisha B'Av, the Jew recalls that God is a steadfast and loving comforter.

Sabbath

"**R**EMEMBER the Sabbath day, to keep it holy. Six days you shall labor, and do all your work; but the seventh day is a Sabbath to the Lord your God."

Of all the Jewish holidays and festivals, Sabbath is the only one mentioned in the Ten Commandments. Set apart by God as a day of calm retreat and reflection, the Sabbath is considered the most important of all holy days by Jews.

Like other Jewish holidays and festivals, Sabbath begins with sunset of the day before. On Friday evening, the home sparkles from a thorough house-cleaning. No matter how poor the family, there is a clean white tablecloth shining with the best plates and tableware. At the head of the table is a decanter of sweet wine with the ceremonial cup waiting beside it. Two loaves of freshly-baked *hallah*—a braided white bread—rest beside the wine. Throughout the home there is an air of expectancy and ease, for Sabbath is at once a restful and festive occasion.

Friday sundown . . . mother lights the candles . . . the Sabbath begins.

The home service begins as the mother of the family lights the Sabbath candles. She praises God for His commandment of rest and peace, and silently asks His blessing upon the home. This is often followed by the reading of verses from Chapter 31 of the Book of Proverbs, in honor of the good wife and mother:

> *A woman of valor, who can find? for her price is above rubies. She looketh well to the ways of her household, and eateth not the bread of idleness . . .*

Then, the father of the family raises his cup and recites the *Kiddush*—the ancient prayer sanctifying the Sabbath. The following is from the Kiddush service in the Reform tradition:

> *Let us praise God with this symbol of joy, and thank Him for the blessings of the past week, for life, health and strength, for home, love, and friendship, for the discipline of our trials and temptations, for the happiness that has come to us out of our labors. Thou hast ennobled us, O God, by the blessings of work, and in love and kindness Thou hast sanctified us by the blessings of rest through the Commandment.*

After this, the father recites a blessing over the wine:

> *Blessed art Thou, O Lord, our God, Ruler of the universe, Who createst the fruit of the vine.*

Then, breaking open the golden hallah loaves, he recites the grace:

> *Blessed art Thou, O Lord, our God, Ruler of the universe, Who bringest forth bread from the earth.*

Finally, over the bowed heads of his family, he asks God's blessing upon the children.

This ceremony launches a traditionally delicious meal, accompanied by special songs and cheerful conversation, for the Sabbath is a time for pleasure as well as prayer and contemplation. The family spirit of devotion on the Sabbath inspires a feeling of love and friendship for all people, and a hope that

Raising the cup for the Kiddush, the ancient prayer sanctifying the Sabbath.

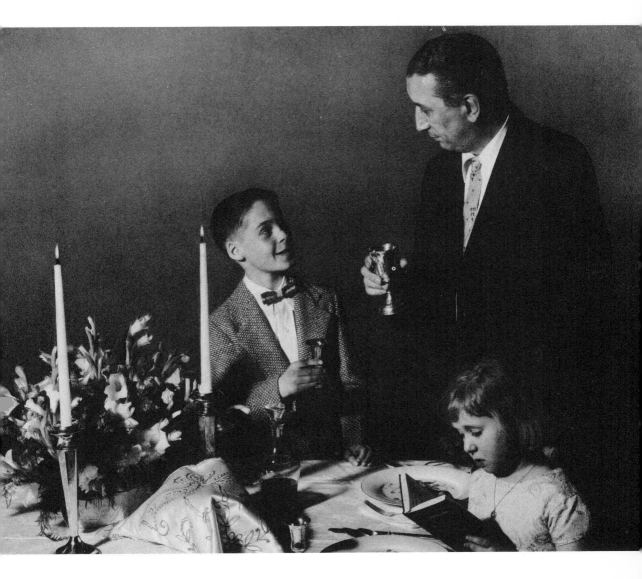

all may share the blessed peace of Sabbath. This hope is reflected in a Sabbath prayer from the synagogue service:

Strengthen the bonds of friendship and fellowship among the inhabitants of all lands. Plant virtue in every soul, and may the love of Thy name hallow every home and every heart. Praised be Thou, O Lord, Giver of Peace.

In Jewish tradition and folklore, the Sabbath is so welcome a guest that it is called "the Queen." Like an honored visitor, the Sabbath Queen is ushered in with joy and singing; *Shalom Aleyhem*—"peace unto you" is the greeting one Jew gives another. It is the greeting he sings as he welcomes the Sabbath.

The departure of the Sabbath is also marked in Orthodox and Conservative synagogues by a special ceremony called *Havdalah,* from the Hebrew root meaning "separation," for the Lord distinguished and set apart the Sabbath from all other days and hallowed it in His name. At this service, a pretty braided and multicolored candle is lit. It demonstrates the many-faceted significance of light. Light is the symbol of the divine. It is a symbol of the divine in man. It is also a symbol of the divine law. On the Sabbath, through the kindling of light, the Jew recalls his responsibility to his God and his fellow men. Precious spices are also sniffed at this Havdalah ceremony. Their fragrance is a reminder of the sweetness of the Sabbath. In Reform congregations, youth groups will frequently conduct their own candlelight Havdalah ceremony.

Today, Jews observe the Sabbath in different ways. Orthodox Jews will not ride on the Sabbath. Work, the exchange of money or financial activity of any kind is forbidden. Conservative and Reform Jews, who interpret the Biblical injunctions more liberally, do not restrict their actions to the same degree.

Asking God's blessing upon the children.

Some Jews go to synagogue or temple service on Friday evenings before supper, some after supper. Others attend services on Saturday morning. But for all Jews, the inner meaning of Sabbath is the same: it is a time for physical relaxation and spiritual renewal.

According to Jewish tradition, the Sabbath provides a foretaste of the days to come. In its joyful calm, people become aware of how beautiful the world may be. Indeed, with its leisure and tranquility, the Sabbath has sustained the Jewish people through many of their most painful periods of history. Today, in a troubled and turbulent world, the Sabbath provides an opportunity for study, contemplation and sociability, and for the peace through which people can realize that the earth of God's handiwork is good—as He judged it good.

Symbols of the Sabbath—the spice box, Havdalah candle and Kiddush cup.

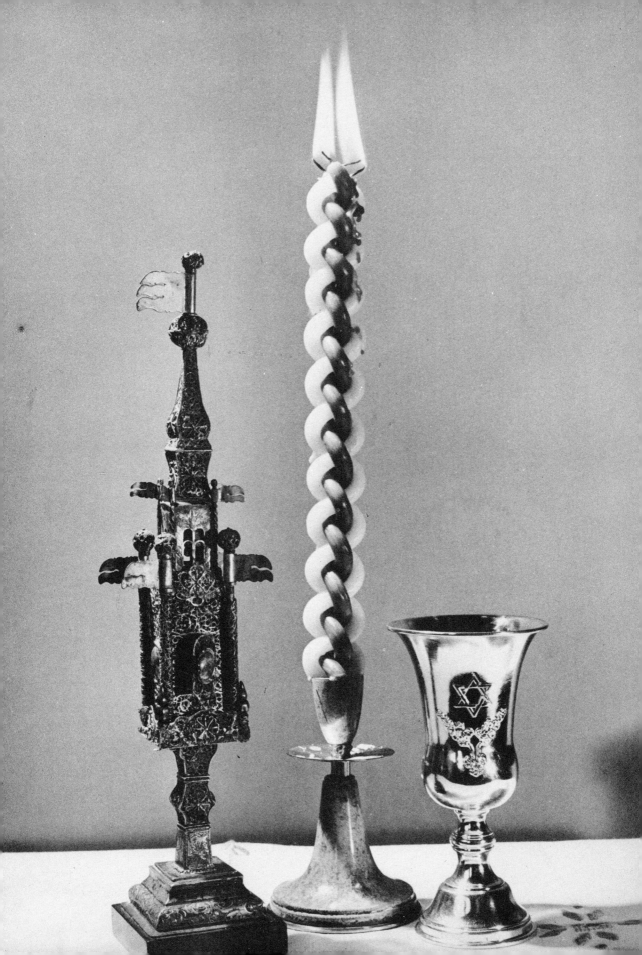

Bar Mitzvah

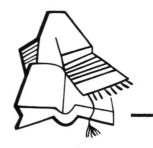

THE greatest day in the life of most young Jewish boys is the day of their *Bar Mitzvah*. Bar Mitzvah means "son of the commandment," which is the Hebrew way of saying he is now responsible for observing God's commandments.

A Jewish boy becomes Bar Mitzvah on his thirteenth birthday, because, according to Jewish tradition, when he reaches that age he is old enough to understand the meaning and purpose of the commandments of the Jewish faith.

Before he becomes Bar Mitzvah, the boy must study the principles and practices of Judaism. In most synagogues he is expected to be able to recite the prayers in Hebrew and to have a good knowledge of the Bible and Jewish history. Generally, he receives this education at the weekday Hebrew school (sometime called *Talmud Torah*) of his synagogue, which holds classes after regular public school hours. He may also study at Sunday School or have a private teacher.

The Bar Mitzvah is generally celebrated in the synagogue on the Sabbath just after a boy's thirteenth birthday. On that Saturday, all of the family's friends and relatives are especially invited to come to the synagogue to join in the celebration. The

Preparing for the Bar Mitzvah requires intensive study.

high point of the service is reached when the lad who is becoming Bar Mitzvah is called to the reading desk to chant the benedictions before and after the reading from the Torah, and to chant a selection from the Prophets called the *Haftorah*.

After this portion of the service, it is customary for the boy to address the congregation briefly and for the rabbi to deliver a special Bar Mitzvah sermon.

When the synagogue services are over, the family of the Bar Mitzvah acts as host to the worshippers at a festive party generally held in the community hall of the synagogue. Sometimes a party is also given at home that night or the next day. Giving gifts to the Bar Mitzvah boy is the general custom.

After he has become Bar Mitzvah, a Jewish boy has all the privileges of an adult synagogue member. He may be counted as one of the ten men (*minyan*) who according to Jewish custom must be present before services can take place; he may be called upon to take part in the reading of the Torah; and he may act as the cantor, if he is able. He also accepts the duty of observing all the ceremonies and customs as well as the ethical laws of his faith.

The Bar Mitzvah ceremony is almost always practiced in Orthodox and Conservative synagogues. In many Reform congregations, too, boys celebrate their Bar Mitzvah although they are also expected to be confirmed when older.

In some congregations a new ceremony has been introduced recently, called *Bath Mitzvah* or "daughter of the commandment." This ceremony is for young girls who have reached the age of thirteen and is somewhat similar to the Bar Mitzvah ceremony. Most often it is held at Sabbath eve services on Friday night.

High point of the Bar Mitzvah—being called to chant the benediction.

Confirmation

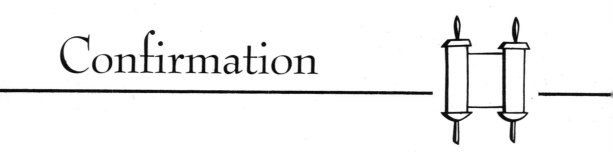

IN a great many synagogues it is the custom for boys and girls to be confirmed on the festival of Shavuoth. Shavuoth has been chosen as the time for confirmation because the young people who are being confirmed renew the promise of their forefathers to observe the teachings of the Torah which were given on Shavuoth. The age at which Jewish children are confirmed varies in different synagogues. Generally confirmation takes place at fifteen or sixteen.

Confirmation comes as the culmination of a rigorous course of study in the beliefs and practices of Judaism. Usually a service of consecration is held on the evening prior to confirmation services on Shavouth morning. The consecration service is limited to the consecrants and their parents. The rabbi speaks to the young people most seriously about their newly acquired responsibilities as members of the faith.

On Shavuoth morning a more public and festive confirmation exercise takes place. The synagogue is decorated with flowers and greens. Sometimes in the procession to the pulpit the

A confirmation class studies the Torah.

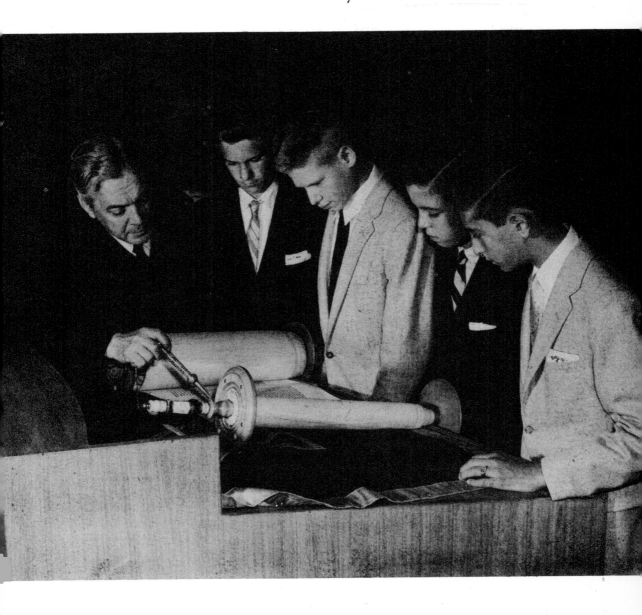

young girls carry flowers to show that Shavuoth is also a harvest festival. In most confirmation ceremonies the reading of the Ten Commandments from the Torah is the central point of the service. The boys and girls who are being confirmed all take part in the services. Some lead in the recitation of the prayers, others speak briefly on the meaning of the Jewish faith and still others may recite selections from the Bible or other Jewish religious works. At the end of the confirmation, the children face the open Ark in which the Torah is kept. The children are then blessed by the rabbi with the ancient Jewish priestly blessing (Numbers 6:22-27):

> *The Lord bless thee, and keep thee;*
> *The Lord make His face to shine upon thee,*
> *And be gracious unto thee;*
> *The Lord lift up His countenance upon thee,*
> *And give thee peace.*

The Synagogue

The Synagogue

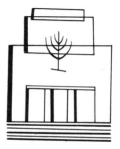

THE Jews did not always worship in synagogues. In ancient days they performed their religious obligations before the "Ark of the Law," which was built to house the holy tablets of the Ten Commandments.

The Ark was kept in a tent or a temporary tabernacle, for the Jews in those days moved about from place to place in their quest for the Promised Land. Later, when they settled in Canaan (Palestine), King Solomon built a magnificient temple on Mount Zion in Jerusalem, with a special room set aside for the Ark.

The Jews worshipped in Solomon's Temple for about 350 years, until 586 B.C.E. In that year Nebuchadnezzar, the king of Babylonia, made war on the Jews, looted the Temple and destroyed it. The Jews lost not only their place of worship, but their homeland, for Nebuchadnezzar carried many of them off to Babylonia as captives. This period is known in Jewish history as "the Exile."

By the time of the Exile, the Jews had already developed many religious observances: the Sabbath, Holy Days, fast days, festival and feast days. These religious customs had become

A section of the Arch of Titus in Rome, showing Jewish captives in the year 70 carrying their Temple menorah to Rome.

part of their everyday lives and signified the ways through which they expressed their faith in God. The Jews refused to abandon these practices in the alien land of Babylonia. Until that time men had given up their gods when their territories were vanquished, or they were forced into exile, and had worshipped the deities of their conquerors. The Jews conceived of God's dominion as unlimited by national or political boundaries. They would not give up their faith even though they were in a strange land. Deprived of their Temple, with its altar and room containing the Holy Ark, deprived of almost all their ritual equipment, they created new ways to worship God. They began to meet in one another's homes, to sing the songs of the Temple on Sabbaths and holy days, to read and discuss the holy scrolls they had salvaged from Jerusalem and to pray for the time when they could return. When the gatherings became too large for private homes, they built special halls for the meetings. By gathering to study God's commandments, they kept faith with Him.

The Jews were permitted to return to Jerusalem after about 50 years of exile. Although they immediately started to build a new Temple on Mount Zion, they realized the value of the study meetings in Babylonia, and continued to gather on the Sabbath to discuss and interpret holy writings. These sessions became so popular that Jews began to congregate on Mondays and Thursdays too, for prayer and study, and soon for daily prayer services. Even in the Temple itself, a special place was set aside for these meetings.

Such a gathering place was called *Beth Knesset* (house of assembly), and the Greeks translated this into *synagoge*. Although the Temple was still regarded as the House of the Lord, the Jews established a great many synagogues throughout Palestine. In fact it was in the synagogue that Jesus

Part of the mosaic floor of the Beth Alpha Synagogue, one of the ancient synagogues recently unearthed in Israel.

preached to his fellow Jews.

By the time of Jesus and Paul, the synagogue served many functions. It was a house of study of the Law and the Prophets. It was a community center for public meetings. It was used for the distribution of charity to the poor, and for the shelter and care of strangers. Like the Temple, the synagogue became securely established as a necessary part of Jewish life.

In the year 70, 600 years after the Jews had returned to Jerusalem from their captivity in Babylonia, the Temple was again destroyed. This time it was the Romans under General Titus who razed it, and again the Jews were driven out of their homes. However, the synagogue helped to hold the Jewish people together in this period of crisis. It housed the word of God, and in it the Jews felt close to Him.

The External Appearance

Synagogues are built in a variety of architectural styles. Whatever their shape or form, however, they will most likely have worked into the outside wall or stained-glass windows, a six-pointed star; this is a *Mogen David* (Shield of David), one of the symbols of Judaism. In place of the Mogen David there may be found a representation of the tablets of the Ten Commandments, or of the burning bush through which God addressed Moses, or of some other precious Jewish symbol. The name of the congregation will usually be inscribed in Hebrew on the facade of the synagogue.

Often, a Biblical quotation will also be inscribed, "Thou shalt love thy neighbor as thyself," and "Do justly, love mercy and walk humbly with thy God," are favored because they express Judaism's universal concern.

So important is learning in the Jewish tradition,
that congregations are instructed to build a
schoolhouse even before a sanctuary.

The Interior

Attached to the right-hand doorpost of the synagogue entrance is a most familiar Jewish symbol—the *mezzuzah*. The mezzuzah is also placed at the entrance of the Jewish home. It is a fragment of rolled parchment in a small case or chamber. The parchment includes the following Biblical verses in Hebrew:

Hear, O Israel, the Lord our God, the Lord is One.
And thou shalt love the Lord thy God with all thy heart,
With all thy soul, and with all thy might,
And these words, which I command thee this day, shall be
*   upon thy heart.*
And thou shalt teach them diligently unto thy children, and
*   shalt talk of them when thou sittest in thy house, and*
*   when thou walkest by the way, and when thou liest*
*   down, and when thou risest up.*
And thou shalt bind them for a sign upon thy hand, and they
*   shall be for frontlets between thine eyes.*
And thou shalt write them upon the doorposts of thy house
*   and upon thy gates. (Deut. 6:49)*

There are many rooms in the synagogue building: classrooms for children and adults and meeting rooms for various leisure-time activities. Now, as before, the synagogue is a gathering place for the Jews of the community.

The sanctuary, where synagogue worship is conducted, generally faces the East.

In the front of the sanctuary there is a raised platform, and in the very center of the platform is the Ark, covered by an embroidered curtain. The Ark and the curtain derive from the Tabernacle of Biblical days, as described in the Bible: "And thou shalt make a veil of blue, and purple, and scarlet and fine

Interior of Mt. Zion Temple, St. Paul, Minnesota.

twisted linen . . . and the veil shall divide unto you between the holy place and the most holy. And thou shalt put the Ark cover upon the Ark of the testimony in the most holy place." (Exodus 26: 31-34)

The figures decorating the Ark curtain are richly allegorical. Like most Jewish ceremonial adornments, they serve to stimulate the imagination as well as please the eye. They recall some significant event in Jewish history, or refer to a passage from the Bible or Jewish literature, or suggest some concept central to Judaism. The embroidered crown on the Ark curtain symbolizes the supremacy of the teachings of God in the Jewish faith. The tablets below the crown represent the Ten Commandments. Two "lions of Judah" may adorn the curtain, symbolizing the ancient tribe of Judah, from which arose King David and King Solomon, and from whose historic kingdom the Jews of today are descended. Other animals may be represented, suggesting the rabbinical injunction: "Be bold as the leopard, fleet as the deer, light as the eagle, and strong as the lion, to do the will of thy Father who is in Heaven."

After the curtain is drawn, the Ark is clearly seen. In the Ark reposes the Torah, a scroll containing the Five Books of Moses. Legend tells us that a Roman emperor once stormed into the Temple of Jerusalem and demanded from the high priest the treasures of the Jews. The priest took the emperor to the "holy of holies," the room containing the Ark, and told him the treasure was inside. The emperor greedily opened the Ark, hoping to find precious jewels or gold. Instead, he found the sacred scrolls of the Law, the Torah. When he realized that the

Shearith Israel (Spanish and Portuguese) Synagogue, New York City. The congregation of this synagogue was the first to be established in the United States, in 1695.

81

Jews regarded a spiritual possession as their most precious treasure, he was so moved that he left the Temple and Jerusalem in peace.

Above the Ark are two tablets with Hebrew letters on them, usually abbreviations of the Ten Commandments. A constantly burning lamp hangs in front of the Ark—the *Ner Tamid* (Eternal Light).

On the platform or dais there is a reading table or desk on which the Torah is placed. There are also two seven-branched candelabra *(menorah)* on the platform, reminiscent of the candles which lit the ancient Temple in Jerusalem, as ordained in the Bible: "And thou shalt make a candlestick of pure gold: of beaten work shall the candlestick be made...and there shall be six branches going out of the sides thereof: three branches of the candlestick out of the one side thereof, and three branches of the candlestick out of the other side thereof . . . and thou shalt make the lamps thereof seven; and they shall light the lamps thereof, to give light over against it." (Exodus 25:31-40)

The dais recalls the famous scribe, Ezra, who established the custom of reading from the sacred writings as a part of the worship service, and used to lecture from a raised platform in the streets of Jerusalem. The unique development of public study as worship—which has since become a concept basic to many other religions—owes much to Ezra.

The Scroll of the Law

When the Ark is opened, we see the Torah scrolls, crowned by their exquisite headpieces. These are finely-worked silver coronets, fashioned with skill and devotion by Jewish artisans.

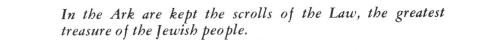

In the Ark are kept the scrolls of the Law, the greatest treasure of the Jewish people.

Their Hebrew name is *rimmonim,* which means "pomegranates"—the rich fruit that is an ancient symbol of life and creativity. As ornament and symbol, the pomegranate appears frequently in Jewish literature and tradition. In the days of the ancient Temple, pomegranates were embroidered on the vestments of the high priest.

On most crowns and rimmonim there are little tinkling bells hanging in various openings, so that a sweet and pleasing sound is heard when the Torah is moved. These, too, call to mind the bells worn by the high priest, as described in the Bible, "a golden bell and pomegranate upon the skirts of the robe around about." (Exodus 28:34) In recent days, the crown has been decorated with other forms and created in different shapes.

When the crown is removed, two rollers or handles are seen. The ends of the parchment on which the Torah is written are attached to these rollers, and by turning the rollers the scroll is opened or closed. The roller is called *Etz Hayyim* (tree of life). The Torah, too, is called "a tree of life to them that hold fast to it." (Proverbs 3:18)

Before the Torah can be unrolled, two other coverings must be removed. First, there is the silver breastplate (*hoshen*). This is a reminder of the special "breastplate of judgment" worn by the high priest when he officiated at the services in the Temple. The breastplate of the high priest was studded with stones of various colors—twelve of them, for the tribes of Israel—in accordance with the Biblical injunction "and thou shalt make a breastplate of judgment, the work of the skillful workman; and shalt set in it settings of stone . . . and the stones shall be according to the names of the children of Israel, twelve according to their names . . . they shall be for the twelve tribes." (Exodus 28:15-21) Some of the Torah breastplates in modern synagogues are still decorated in this fashion. For the past several hundred years, however, Jewish craftsmen have engraved other significant designs on the breastplates. Underneath the breastplate is a mantle that encases the scroll like a robe. It may be made of silk or velvet or fine brocade. It may be elaborately embroidered.

As we know, the Torah consists of the Five Books of Moses (Pentateuch). A specific portion is read each week at the Sabbath service, and in traditional synagogues, also on Monday and Thursday. These portions are so divided that in the course of one year the whole of the Torah will be read. A special holiday marks the occasion on which the scroll is completed, re-rolled, and the reading begun again from Genesis. This holiday is called Simhath Torah (the rejoicing over the Torah), signifying man's joy in the continual discovery of God's message.

In traditional synagogues the Torah portion is chanted to the tune of ancient melodies which are preserved through a system of notes called "trope." The Jewish system of trope existed long before the present system of writing musical notes on a five-line bar. The trope are symbols and notations found above and below the words in the Hebrew Bible. Each of these symbols has a certain musical value, and since the notations are fixed, the tunes of the Biblical and prophetic portions have been transmitted from generation to generation.

The Torah reader uses a *yod* (hand), which is a special rod or pointer to keep his place. Like every article connected with the Torah it is tastefully designed, in keeping with other ornaments.

Torah scrolls are handmade and handwritten by a *sofer* (scribe). A sofer must have scholarly training for his labor of devotion. He must follow very definite rules regarding the size of the margins, the length of lines and the number of letters printed on a line. For the last three hundred years most of the scribes received their training in Eastern Europe, especially in

Poland, where large numbers of Jews used to live. But the Nazis killed most of the Jews in Europe, and destroyed the Jewish centers of learning there. Although there are some skilled scribes in the United States, most of the Torah scrolls are now prepared in Israel.

Great care is taken in the making of the parchment itself. Only the skins of *kosher* (ritually clean) animals are used. The parchment is treated with various chemicals to make it durable, and sewn together with the threads of dried tendons.

Throughout their history the Jews have treated the Torah with reverence and love, and their customs as well as their religious rituals reflect this abiding respect. One such custom, still observed by some Jews, is introducing the child to his first religious instruction by placing a drop of honey on the first page of the Bible and asking the child to kiss it. Thus, God's law is shown to be sweet and, from his very earliest years, the Jewish child is taught to love and respect it.

The Eternal Light

Light, as a symbol of the divine, has played an important role in the writ and ritual of Judaism. The Eternal Light burns perpetually before the synagogue Ark, as ordained in the Bible: "And thou shalt command the children of Israel, that they bring unto thee pure olive oil beaten for the light, to cause the lamp to burn continually . . . it shall be a statute forever throughout their generations . . ." (Exodus 27:20-21)

The Jewish festival of Hanukkah dramatically illustrates the

In every synagogue, there is a Ner Tamid or Eternal Light, which is never extinguished.

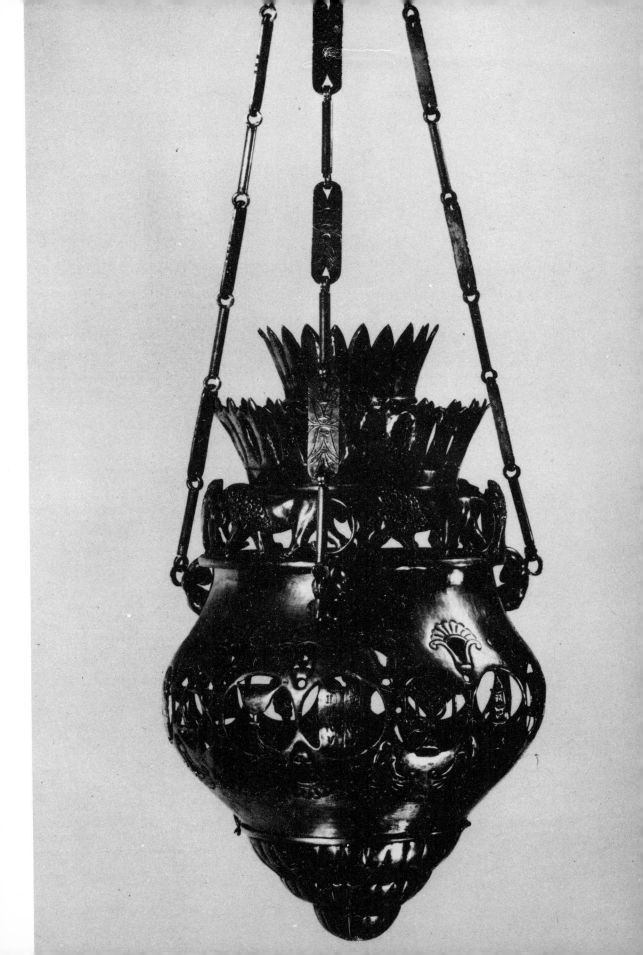

significance of light. When Judah Maccabee liberated the ancient Temple for the Jews, he found the Ner Tamid unlit, and all the cruses (jars containing special oil) destroyed save one. Yet this single cruse of oil nourished the Eternal Light for eight days and nights. Today, the Jews commemorate this miracle by lighting one additional candle on each of the eight days of Hanukkah.

The ceremony of candle-lighting pervades Jewish ritual. In the home, as well as in the synagogue, candles are lit on every Sabbath eve, and on many of the Jewish festivals. The significance of this tradition is revealed by the following selection from the Sabbath candle-lighting ceremony in the Reform synagogue service:

> *Light is the symbol of the Divine. "The Lord is my light and my salvation."*
> *Light is the symbol of the divine in man. "The spirit of man is the light of the Lord."*
> *Light is the symbol of Israel's mission. "I the Lord have set thee for a covenant of the people, for a light unto the nations."*

The Synagogue Service

A synagogue is more than a storehouse of memories; it is a living house of prayer, to which Jews come to commune with God. Just as all Christian churches do not follow the same ritual, so there are different patterns of worship in synagogues. The Bible does not prescribe a specific worship service, nor does the Jewish faith empower any single authority to establish

> *". . . Thou hast preserved us and sustained us and brought us to this day."*

rules of worship. Each congregation, therefore, can fashion its own service. However, though the practices in modern synagogues are somewhat varied, there are certain basic prayers around which the service is constructed, serving as a unifying bond among Jewish communities everywhere.

The arrangement of these basic prayers is almost as old as the synagogue itself. The men of the Great Assembly—the prophets, sages, scribes and teachers who led the people in the centuries after their return from Babylonia—established the lines on which Jewish congregational and individual prayer have moved ever since. These men made the *b'raha* (blessing or benediction) the unit of Jewish prayer, each blessing beginning with the Hebrew words for "Blessed art Thou, O Lord our God, King of the Universe."

The men of the Great Assembly also established the congregational form of prayer. Although the Jew addresses God personally and individually, through congregational readings and responses he experiences a sense of fellowship with his brethren and with all mankind. This is heightened by the inclusive phrasing of the prayers themselves which ask blessings for all men more often than for the individual: "Let the beauty of Thy holiness shine into our hearts, that we may grow more steadfast in our faith and in our love of Thee and of our fellow men."

In the period after the destruction of the Temple, great rabbis continued to compose prayers and hymns. The free poetic and liturgical expressions of the greatest creative minds in the Jewish community were added to the core service. Finally, in the ninth century all of these prayers were gathered together into one collection, a *Siddur* (order—from the same Hebrew root as *seder*).

However, the need to express the deepest longings of the heart in prayer continued to inspire Jews to revise and add to their prayer service. Varying traditions began to develop in different lands where the people learned to pray in words composed by their beloved teachers.

About a century ago, other marked changes in the method of synagogue worship occurred, at the time known as the Emancipation. At that time, democratic governments were first being established, and the Jews were granted equal opportunities before the law. Heretofore, under the rule of feudal lords and despotic kings, the Jews had been denied many rights. As a result of their new freedom, they emerged from ghetto restrictions and shared ideas and practices with their neighbors of other faiths. This experience, plus the influence of new scientific knowledge that was then changing man's way of thinking, led to a revision in Jewish religious practice. Some prayers were changed. Some congregations decided to add organ music and a mixed choir of male and female voices to accompany the cantor. Other congregations decided to translate the prayers from Hebrew into the language spoken in the country in which they lived, so that everyone could understand the service. Still others decided to do away with the restrictions which kept men and women in separate sections during the prayer services.

The congregations that brought about these new practices were called Reform—because of the "reforms" they instituted. The congregations that observed all the traditional practices without change were called Orthodox. The Orthodox leaders believed that the traditional customs of prayer were holy and that men had no right to make arbitrary changes. Reform Jews, on the other hand, asserted that the religious service was intended to inspire man in every generation and to afford him the experience of worship. Man had the right to change the service so long as he maintained the essential spirit of devotion to God.

In time, there developed a third group of congregations

called Conservative, which kept most of the traditional practices yet introduced some changes. While Conservative congregations have changed many Orthodox practices, generally they have not instituted as many innovations as the Reform congregations.

These differences in worship may be seen in American synagogues. In Orthodox and Conservative congregations, the men wear a *yarmulka* (head-covering) during prayer, following the manner in which people in the Near East still show respect and reverence. In addition, the Orthodox and Conservative Jews wear a prayer shawl with fringes, called a *Tallith*. Under the influence of the European and American customs of dress, however, Reform congregations have given up wearing yarmulkas or prayer shawls during the service, although some rabbis in Reform temples still wear the traditional vestments.

Reform and many Conservative synagogues permit organ music and choirs of male and female voices. They also permit families to sit together during worship, and they have added many English translations to the prayer service. Orthodox synagogues, however, do not sanction instrumental music at prayer services. Such prohibition is considered a sign of mourning for the destruction of the revered Temple in Jerusalem and serves to distinguish the synagogue from that Temple. Also, in the Orthodox tradition, the playing of music is considered a violation of Sabbath and Holy Day injunctions. Orthodox synagogues still maintain separate sections for men and women, as was the practice during the days of the Temple in Zion.

Despite these differences, Orthodox, Conservative and Reform Jews still have a great common tradition of religious practice, which is basic and fundamental to Jewish religious

Inscribed for all time, the age-old Jewish prayer of faith.

שמע ישראל
יהוה אלהינו
יהוה אחד

Hear, O Israel: The Lord
our God, the Lord is one.

belief. In all congregations, for example, the central prayer is the *Shema,* the age-old Jewish espousal of faith, which is recited in Hebrew: "Hear, O Israel, the Lord our God, the Lord is One."

In all synagogues, the congregation stands in reverence when important blessings are said, when the Ark is opened, and when the holy Torah is brought forth.

At all Sabbath and appropriate holiday prayer services, there are readings from the Scriptures—a portion from the Books of Moses and a selection from the Prophets or Writings—again stressing the vital connection between instruction and prayer in the synagogue.

All congregations participate actively in services. The people say prayers in unison, engage in responsive reading with the rabbi, sometimes sing or chant along with the cantor, and respond with Hebrew phrases of gratitude when the rabbi or cantor recites a prayer or offers blessings to the Lord for His gifts to mankind. There is a time for the congregation to engage in silent devotion, and a time for each individual to utter his own personal prayers to God. All synagogues are open for daily prayer. Orthodox and Conservative synagogues conduct services morning and evening every day of the year.

The Cantor and the Rabbi

The earliest records of Jewish prayer acknowledge the important place of music. In the days of the Temple in Jerusalem, the services always included the chanting of sacred songs by a specially trained group of temple priests, usually accompanied

Jewish Chapel at Brandeis University, Waltham, Massachusetts

by musicians. In the synagogues of today a cantor sings the prayers, often accompanied by a choir, and sometimes by an organ.

There are schools of sacred music that still teach the traditional chants, transmitted from generation to generation. In the course of time, new melodies have been added to the traditional ones.

The rabbi is the religious leader of the congregation, directing the services, generally with the assistance of a cantor. Although he leads the prayers and delivers the sermon, he does not act as intermediary between man and God. All Jews commune directly with God, and all, including the rabbi, are responsible to Him for their individual acts.

Although the rabbi now devotes his entire energies to the spiritual needs of the community, the rabbinate was not always a full-time vocation. In ancient times, the people simply appointed the most respected scholar in the community to guide them. He made his living like other people, by working in the fields, or at a trade or profession. He was called *rabbi,* which means "teacher," as a mark of respect for his learning, knowledge and piety.

As the synagogue became the very center of life in the Jewish community, seminaries were established to train people for the rabbinate. Today the title "Rabbi" is reserved for properly ordained graduates of such schools.

In America there are eight large seminaries. These schools possess the largest collection of Jewish books and ceremonial articles to be found anywhere in the world. Rabbinical students are admitted into training after they have acquired their college degrees. They then undergo a rigorous four to six-year period of theological study and spiritual preparation. Rabbis are encouraged to marry and raise a family.

The Church and the Synagogue

By this time it is clear that there are many similarities between a church and a synagogue service. In the church there are also congregational prayers, responsive readings, the recitation of psalms, opportunities for silent meditation, and a sermon. Instruction is also a part of Christian devotion.

It is quite understandable that there are similarities, for the earliest Christians were Jews, and some of the traditional Jewish customs have been carried over into Christianity.

Like the synagogues, churches are also centers of community life, humming with activity the year round. Ministers and priests, like rabbis, are active participants in the social life of the community, and spiritual leaders of their congregations.

There are many differences, of course—differences in ritual and ceremony, in the choice and order of the prayers, and in the meanings given to such symbols as wine, wafer, candles, palm leaves, water and religious vestments. There are also differences in the way the congregation worships. But in all faiths there is a devotion to God and a desire to live in harmony with His ways. Through knowledge of other faiths, we learn to respect differences and strengthen our own respective faiths.

Here in America, we do not let our different beliefs keep us from living in peace and harmony with our neighbor. All our religions insist that we respect the dignity of man, and treat our neighbor as a brother. We are all created by one God. This religious concept of the brotherhood of man under the fatherhood of God is basic to our American democracy. It is the idea that has enabled Americans of many races, religions and ethnic origins to work together and to build a just society. Each individual, in his own way, has contributed to America, and it is the contributions of all that have made America strong. *"God hears prayers in many tongues, and they are all sweet in His ears."*

EXPLANATORY NOTES

THE JEWISH FESTIVALS AND THEIR BIBLICAL SOURCE

Passover, Shavuoth and Succoth are the three great holidays described in the Bible as *pilgrimage festivals*. On each of these occasions there was a harvest celebration and the Jewish people were instructed to make a pilgrimage to Jerusalem, if they could, in order to offer their thanksgiving. There, before the Temple, would take place a magnificent procession accompanied by the singing of Psalms and musical responses from the priestly choir. Each of these holidays, however, also embodies historical and ethical associations. Thus, Passover celebrates man's right to freedom from slavery; Shavuoth, the giving of the Ten Commandments; and Succoth, man's reliance upon the Almighty.

Rosh Hashanah and Yom Kippur are also enjoined by Biblical command; the observance of the Sabbath is proclaimed in the Ten Commandments.

Purim and Hanukkah are holidays of historic connotation and their scriptural sources are to be found outside of the Pentateuch. Purim is described in the Book of Esther and the tale of Hanukkah is related in the Book of Maccabees.

For the source of Lag B'Omer, Tisha B'Av and Hamishah Asar Bishvat, the reader may consult post-Biblical writings.

Pronunciation of Hebrew

Just as the pronunciation of English is different in various parts of the United States, the pronunciation of Hebrew also varies slightly from country to country. As it is spoken today in the land of Israel and in most of the Mediterranean countries, Hebrew is pronounced in the fashion known as *Sephardic*. In most northern and eastern European countries and in most synagogues in the United States, the pronunciation used is called *Ashkenazic*. The differences are mainly in the pronunciation of the vowels. Since the Sephardic pronunciation has become the accepted one in present-day spoken Hebrew, in this book we have given the English spelling of Herbew words which would most closely be equivalent to the Sephardic pronunciation, except where the force of custom dictated otherwise.

In the Hebrew words used in this book, a reasonably close approximation to correct Hebrew pronunciation will be achieved if the following values are given to the vowel sound:

a — as in father
ā — as in made
e — as in bed
ee — as in see
i — as in him
o — as in rope
u — as in rude

The values to be given to the consonants are the same as in English with the exception of the dotted *h* for which there is no equivalent found in the English language. This is a guttural *h* and has a sound approximating the German *ch* in *ich*.

In the Ashkenazic pronunciation, all words ending in *th* or *t* are pronounced as if they ended with an *s*. In present-day spoken Hebrew, words ending in a final *t* or *th* are pronounced as if they ended with a *t*.

The Jewish Calendar

The religious calendar which governs the dates of the Jewish holidays is based on an ancient system of computing time. Unlike the civil calendar, the Jewish calendar takes into consideration the lunar as well as the solar cycle. Thus, Jewish holidays begin in the evening when the sun sets instead of at daybreak when the sun rises. Jewish holidays do not always fall on the same civil calendar date each year, for the lunar cycle does not have as many days each month as does the solar cycle. Thus, the Jewish calendar falls behind the civil calendar until such time as a "leap month" is added to it to make up for the time lapse. The Jewish calendar allegedly began its count with Abraham's journey into Palestine. This accounts for the difference in the year between the Jewish and civil calendar.

Jewish Denominations

There are three Jewish denominations in the United States. They are the Reform, Conservative and Orthodox. All three groups are almost equal in size and all their congregations have been expanding rapidly in this recent period. In general, they all draw their inspiration from the same Biblical and rabbinical writings and they hold in common many ideas concerning God, right and wrong, and the destiny of the Jewish people. They differ, however, on the place of the law in Judaism, particularly the laws dealing with rites and ceremonies.

ORTHODOX JEWS believe that all the laws—both the ethical and ritualistic—to be found in the Bible and the Talmud are holy and can be changed only through limited and prescribed methods of reinterpretation. Certain great rabbinical leaders are given the right to make such reinterpretations. Orthodox Jews faithfully maintain the ancient patterns of religious practice and they hold firmly to traditional, basic beliefs. They suggest that it has been just such devotion to the historic patterns of Judaism that has enabled it to survive through the centuries.

REFORM JEWS do not believe that all the laws in the Bible and rabbinical literature were revealed at one moment. They hold that these laws were developed in the course of years by inspired men who attempted to translate God's will into life. Reform Jews insist that this process of growth and development must continue. They emphasize that the ethical and social ideals of religion are more important than the rituals and ceremonies by which these ideals are expressed. Thus, Reform Jews have felt free to change many of the outward rites of Judaism in order to meet the changed conditions of a modern day. But they have also created new ceremonies which are rapidly being adopted by all Jewish denominations in America.

CONSERVATIVE JEWS believe that law is important but they also believe that the rabbis should be willing to change the law more rapidly in order to meet the new conditions of modern times. Conservative Jews thus tend to maintain more of the rituals than do Reform Jews but less strictly than Orthodox Jews. They insist that the discipline of law is important in maintaining the Jewish community in its faith, but they have encouraged their leaders to be more liberal in reinterpreting the traditional law.

HOLIDAY CALENDAR

	1957-58 (5718)	1958-59 (5719)	1959-60 (5720)	1960-61 (5721)	1961-62 (5722)
*ROSH HASHANAH	SEPT. 26-27	SEPT. 15-16	OCT. 3-4	SEPT. 22-23	SEPT. 11-12
YOM KIPPUR	OCT. 5	SEPT. 24	OCT. 12	OCT. 1	SEPT. 20
*SUCCOTH (1st day)	OCT. 10	SEPT. 29	OCT. 17	OCT. 6	SEPT. 25
HOSHANA RABBA	OCT. 16	OCT. 5	OCT. 23	OCT. 12	OCT. 1
SHEMINI ATZERETH	OCT. 17	OCT. 6	OCT. 24	OCT. 13	OCT. 2
SIMHATH TORAH	OCT. 18	OCT. 7	OCT. 25	OCT. 14	OCT. 3
HANUKKAH	DEC. 18-25	DEC. 7-14	DEC. 26-JAN. 2	DEC. 14-21	DEC. 3-10
HAMISHAH ASAR BISHVAT	FEB. 5	JAN. 24	FEB. 13	FEB. 1	JAN. 20
PURIM	MAR. 6	MAR. 24	MAR. 13	MAR. 2	MAR. 20
*PESAH (1st day)	APR. 5	APR. 23	APR. 12	APR. 1	APR. 19
*PESAH (7th day)	APR. 11	APR. 29	APR. 18	APR. 7	APR. 25
LAG B'OMER	MAY 8	MAY 26	MAY 15	MAY 4	MAY 22
*SHAVUOTH	JUNE 25	JUNE 12	JUNE 1	JUNE 23	JUNE 8
TISHA B'AV	JULY 27	AUG. 13	AUG. 2	JULY 23	AUG. 9

	1962-63 (5723)	1963-64 (5724)	1964-65 (5725)	1965-66 (5726)	1966-67 (5727)
*ROSH HASHANAH	SEPT. 29-30	SEPT. 19-20	SEPT. 7-8	SEPT. 27-28	SEPT. 15-16
YOM KIPPUR	OCT. 8	SEPT. 28	SEPT. 16	OCT. 6	SEPT. 24
*SUCCOTH (1st day)	OCT. 13	OCT. 3	SEPT. 21	OCT. 11	SEPT. 29
HOSHANA RABBA	OCT. 19	OCT. 9	SEPT. 27	OCT. 17	OCT. 5
SHEMINI ATZERETH	OCT. 20	OCT. 10	SEPT. 28	OCT. 18	OCT. 6
SIMHATH TORAH	OCT. 21	OCT. 11	SEPT. 29	OCT. 19	OCT. 7
HANUKKAH	DEC. 22-29	DEC. 11-18	NOV. 30-DEC. 7	DEC. 19-26	DEC. 8-15
HAMISHAH ASAR BISHVAT	JAN. 9	JAN. 29	JAN. 18	FEB. 5	JAN. 26
PURIM	MAR. 10	FEB. 27	MAR. 18	MAR. 6	MAR. 26
*PESAH (1st day)	APR. 9	MAR. 28	APR. 17	APR. 5	APR. 25
*PESAH (7th day)	APR. 15	APR. 3	APR. 23	APR. 11	MAY 1
LAG B'OMER	MAY 12	APR. 30	MAY 20	MAY 8	MAY 28
*SHAVUOTH	MAY 29	MAY 17	JUNE 6	MAY 25	JUNE 14
TISHA B'AV	JULY 30	JULY 19	AUG. 8	JULY 26	AUG. 15

* Orthodox and Conservative congregations celebrate two days, Reform one day only.

Glossary of Hebrew Words

Glossary of Hebrew Words

AFIKOMEN (a-fee-kó-men)

> from the Greek word for "dessert." The piece of unleavened bread which is hidden away during the Passover meal and eaten at the completion of the meal.

BAR MITZVAH (bar mítz-vah)

> literally, "son of the commandment." A Jewish boy becomes bar mitzvah on his thirteenth birthday, when he is considered old enough to undertake the religious responsibilities of an adult male.

BATH MITZVAH (bat mítz-vah)

> literally, "daughter of the commandment." The same ceremony as bar mitzvah, except for Jewish girls, and observed usually in Conservative and Reform congregations.

BEDIKATH HAMETZ (be-dee-kát ha-métz)

> "The search for leaven"—referring to the custom in Orthodox and Conservative homes, observed on the eve of Passover, to seek out and set aside all food articles containing leaven.

BETH KNESSET (bāt knés-set)

> literally, "house of gathering." The Hebrew word for a synagogue.

B'RAHA (b'rahá)

> the Hebrew word for blessing or benediction. The traditional Hebrew blessing always begins: "Blessed art Thou, O Lord our God, Ruler of the Universe . . ."

DREYDEL (drắd'l)

> a four-sided top, used in a game that Jewish children play at Hanukkah. It is a game of put

and take. Using nuts or candies, every participant puts one into the "pot." The children then take turns spinning the dreydel. If it comes to N, the player gets nothing; G, he takes all; H he takes half; SH he puts one in. These four letters refer to the Hebrew words, Nes Gadol, Haya, Sham.

ETHROG (és-rog)

 a citron, or fruit resembling a lemon, which is used in the celebration of Succoth.

ETZ HAYYIM (etz hay-éem)

literally, "tree of life." Designates the wooden rollers to which the ends of the Torah scrolls are attached.

GEFULTE FISH (ge-fíl-te)

a mixed fish dish, usually including carp, which is traditionally served on the Sabbath and holidays.

GREGGER (grég-ger)

 a noisemaker used in the celebration of Purim.

HAD GADYAH (had gad-yáh)

"One Kid," the title of a jolly tune sung at the conclusion of the Passover Seder ceremony.

HAFTORAH (haf-tór-ah)

a selection from the Prophets which the Jewish boy reads and chants when he becomes bar mitzvah.

HAGGADAH (hag-gád-ah)

literally, "story"; the Passover haggadah tells the story of how the Israelites were freed from

111

slavery in Egypt. It is read each year during the Seder ceremony.

HALLAH (hál-lah)

the loaf of Sabbath bread, a white bread generally baked in a braided shape.

HAMANTASHEN (háman-tashen)

three-cornered pastries filled with poppy seeds or prunes; traditionally served at Purim.

HAMISHAH ASAR BISHVAT (ham-ee-shá asár bish-vát)

the fifteenth day of the Hebrew month of Shvat; Jewish arbor day, generally observed by tree-planting ceremonies.

HANUKKAH (hán-u-kah)

"dedication," a holiday commemorating the liberation and the rededication of the ancient Temple in Jerusalem by Judah Maccabee and his followers.

HAROSETH (har-ó-set)

a mixture of apples, nuts, cinnamon and wine, which is eaten at the Passover Seder ceremony, representing the mortar with which the Jews made bricks when they were slaves in the land of Pharaoh.

HAVDALAH (hav-dá-lah)

"separation," a ceremony held Saturday at sunset in Orthodox and Conservative congregations, marking the separation of the Sabbath from the other days of the week.

HOL-HAMOED (hol ha-mo-éd)

designates the weekday days which follow the first two days of Succoth.

112

HOSHANA RABBA (ho-shána ráb-ba)

a prayer for forgiveness uttered by the congregation during the Succoth celebration. It is also the name of the seventh day of the Succoth holiday.

HOSHEN (ho-shen)

designates both the breastplate worn by the high priest in the ancient Temple, and the breastplate which covers the mantle over the Torah scrolls.

KIDDUSH (kíd-dush)

literally, "sanctification." This is a special prayer sanctifying the Sabbath and other holidays. It is said over a cup of wine.

KOL NIDRE (kol níd-rä)

this is a prayer, generally sung by the cantor, that opens the synagogue service on Yom Kippur evening. It is a prayer to God asking forgiveness for vows that have been made to Him and not kept.

KOSHER (kósh-er)

the term used for designating animals which are ritually clean according to traditional Jewish standards.

LAG B'OMER (lag b'ómer)

a holiday commemorating the struggle of the great Rabbi Akiba and his disciple Simeon Bar Yohai, for freedom. The holiday comes thirty-three days after Passover and is generally celebrated with picnics and outings.

LATKES (lát-kes)

these are crisp potato pancakes, generally served during the celebration of Hanukkah.

113

LULAV (lú-lav)

a branch made of palm, willow and myrtle leaves, and used in the celebration of Succoth. During the synagogue services, this branch is waved in all directions symbolizing that God is to be found everywhere.

MA NISHTANAH (ma nish-tá-nah)

the opening words of the four questions asked by a young child at the Passover Seder ceremony:

Why is this night different from all other nights? On all other nights we eat bread or matzoth. Why on this night do we eat only matzoth? On all other nights we eat all kinds of herbs. Why on this night do we eat only bitter herbs? On all other nights we do not dip herbs in any condiment. Why on this night do we dip twice, greens in salt water and bitter herbs in haroseth? On all other nights we may sit at the table either erect or leaning. Why on this night do we recline?

MAROR (mar-ór)

designates the bitter herbs which are eaten during the Passover Seder, reminding Jews of the bitterness of slavery.

MATZOTH (mát-zos)

the flat, unleavened bread which is eaten during the Passover holiday. These wafers commemorate the flight of the ancient Israelites from Egypt, when the Hebrew slaves fled so quickly that they did not have time for the dough of their bread to rise. *Matzah* (mát-zah) refers to a single wafer.

MEGILLAH (me-gíl-lah)

a special scroll of parchment. The word generally refers to the Book of Esther, which is read at the time of the celebration of Purim.

114

MENORAH (men-ó-rah)

> the Hebrew word for candelabra. There are two kinds of menorah: a seven-branched candlestick which is used for regular worship, and an eight-branched candlestick which is used in the celebration of Hanukkah.

MEZZUZAH (mez-zú-zah)

> a tiny scroll of parchment housed in a small wooden or metal case. The parchment contains scriptural readings, and the mezzuzah is placed on the outside doorposts of Jewish homes and synagogues, in accordance with Biblical injunction.

MINYAN (mín-yan)

> any ten adult Jewish males can start a congregation at any time and at any place. This quorum of ten is called a minyan.

MOGEN DAVID (ma-gén da-veéd)

> literally, "shield of David," referring to the six-pointed star which has become a symbol of the Jewish religion.

NER TAMID (ner tam-eéd)

> the Eternal Light which burns continuously before the Ark housing the sacred scrolls of Judaism.

NES GADOL HAYA SHAM (nes gadól hayá sham)

> this Hebrew expression means "a great miracle happened there," and refers to the rededication of the ancient Temple in Jerualem, when it was liberated by Judah Maccabee and his army. The first letter of each word appears on the four sides of the dreydel.

ONEG SHABBAT (ó-neg sha-bát)

> "the pleasure of the Sabbath," the title given to the late Friday evening or Saturday afternoon repast and festivities celebrating the Sabbath.

PESAH (pá-sah)

> the Hebrew word for Passover, the spring festival of freedom.

PURIM (pú-rim)

> "lots"—a joyous holiday commemorating the courage of Queen Esther in saving the Jewish people from death at the hands of the wicked Haman, who had cast lots in order to choose the day of destruction of the Jews.

RIMMONIM (rim-mon-eém)

> the Hebrew word for "pomegranates," designating the silver crowns which top the Torah scrolls.

ROSH HASHANAH (rosh ha-shá-nah)

> "first of the year." This is the Jewish New Year, one of the two high holy days of the Jewish religion.

SEDER (sá-der)

> the family worship service and meal which constitutes the home Passover ceremony.

SEFER TORAH (sa-fer tó-rah)

> the Torah scrolls, containing the five books of Moses, sacred in the Jewish religion. In addition to the Pentateuch, the word Torah means learning and signifies the ethical way of life.

SHALOM ALEYHEM (sha-lóm a-lay-hem)

> "peace unto you." A greeting of welcome in the Jewish tradition; it is expressed in song on Friday evening, when the celebrant greets the coming of the Sabbath.

116

SHAMOS (shá-mes)

> "helper." Refers to the helper candle used to light the other candles during the Hanukkah celebration.

SHAVUOTH (sha-vu-ót)

> a thanksgiving and harvest feast, also commemorating the giving of the Ten Commandments on Mount Sinai. In many synagogues it has become the custom to confirm Jewish young people on Shavuoth. Shavuoth means "weeks" and the holiday known as the Feast of Weeks is celebrated seven weeks after Passover.

SHEMA (sh'má)

> the first word of the Hebew prayer which is the watchword of the Jewish religion and its central concept: "Hear O Israel, the Lord our God, the Lord is One."

SHEMINI ATZERETH (sh'mi-neé a-zér-et)

> the "eighth day of solemn assembly" of the Succoth holiday.

SHOFAR (shó-far)

> the ram's horn blown on the New Year and Yom Kippur.

SIDDUR (sid-dúr)

> this is an "order" or collection of Jewish prayers which were gathered together in the ninth century and provide the basis for most Jewish worship service today.

SIMHATH TORAH (sím-has tór-ah)

> the day of "rejoicing over the Torah." This day celebrates the end of a year's reading from the Torah, and the beginning of the year's reading anew, starting with the first chapter of Genesis.

SOFER (so-fér)

the Hebrew word for a scribe, the man who handwrites the sacred Torah scrolls.

SUCCAH (suc-cáh)

a booth made of branches, decorated with fruits and flowers.

SUCCOTH (suc-cót)

a thanksgiving festival which lasts for nine days. During this time many Jews eat their meals in a succah.

TALLITH (tál-lis)

a fringed prayer shawl which is worn by many Jews when they pray.

TISHA B'AV (ti-shá b'áv)

the ninth day in the Hebrew month of Av. It is a day of mourning and lamentation commemorating a series of catastrophies in Jewish history.

YARMULKA (yár-mul-ka)

a skull cap worn by many Jews.

YIZKOR (yíz-kor)

the traditional Hebrew prayer in memoriam for the departed.

YOD (yad)

literally, a "hand"; it is the pointer, usually made of precious metal, which is used when the Torah is read in the synagogue.

YOM KIPPUR (yom kíp-pur)

the "Day of Atonement," when Jews seek forgiveness for their sins and "at-one-ment" with God. The most solemn day of the Jewish calendar.

118

THE PHOTOGRAPHS